J. Severino Croatto

Biblical Hermeneutics

Toward a Theory of Reading as the Production of Meaning

Translated from the Spanish by
Robert R. Barr

ORBIS BOOKS
Maryknoll, New York 10545

Originally published as *Hermenéutica bíblica: Para una teoría de la lectura como producción sentido,* © 1984 by Asociación Ediciones la Aurora, Buenos Aires, Argentina

English translation © 1987 by Orbis Books, Maryknoll, NY 10545
All rights reserved
Manufactured in the United States of America

Manuscript editor and indexer: William E. Jerman

Except where otherwise indicated, scripture quotations are from the *New American Bible* (NAB). (NEB = *New English Bible*)

Library of Congress Cataloging in Publication Data

Croatto, J. Severino (José Severino)
  Biblical hermeneutics.

  Translation of: Hermenéutica biblica.
  Bibliography: p.
  Includes index.
  1. Bible—Hermeneutics. I. Title.
BS476.C7613   1987   220.6'01   87-12314
ISBN 0-88344-583-2
ISBN 0-88344-582-4 (pbk.)

Dedicated to all who make their lives
a living witness of the word of God,
rereading it from the vantage point
of their commitment to the dispossessed.

Contents

Preface   ix

Introduction   1
    Philosophical Hermeneutics: Three Major Phases   2
        1. The Modern Era   3
        2. The Middle Ages   4
        3. Philo of Alexandria   4
    Five Approaches to the Bible   5
        1. Present Reality as Primary "Text"   5
        2. Concordism   6
        3. Historico-Critical Methods   7
        4. Structural Analysis   9
        5. Hermeneutics   9

Chapter 1
From Semiotics to Hermeneutics   13
    Language as System and as Event   13
    Language as Text and as Writing   15
    Reading as Production of Meaning:
        The Hermeneutic Act   20
    Implications of Reading as Production of Meaning   25
        Transformation and Its Concealment   25
        Textual Dependency   29
        Appropriation of Meaning   30
        The Hermeneutic Function of Distantiation   34

Chapter 2
Praxis and Interpretation   36
    From Event to Text   36
        Foundational Events   39

    From Closure to Polysemy   *40*
    Tradition   *41*
    Canon   *43*
    Inspiration   *46*
    Canonicity and Re-creation   *47*
  The "Forward" of a Text   50
  Intratextuality   54
    New Meaning in New Totalizations   *54*
    The Bible: A Single Text   *56*
  To Whom Does the Bible "Pertain" and "Belong"?   60

Chapter 3
Exegesis and Eisegesis   **66**
  A Rereading of the Bible: Part of Its Total
    Message   66
  Updating the Bible? Illumination of Reality?   69
  Closed or Open Revelation?   71
  The Language of Faith   76
  Recontextualization of the Biblical Kerygma   79
  Some Objections   80
  Conclusion   82

Notes   **84**

Glossary   **89**

Scripture Index   **91**

General Index   **93**

Preface

The point of departure of this work is the conviction that the Bible is not a closed deposit that has already "said" it all. It is a text that speaks to us in the present. But it speaks as a *text*—not as a generic exhortation to spur our decision-making. The tension between a fixed text in a cultural milieu that is no longer ours and a living word capable of forging history can be resolved only by a fertile *rereading*. This is the problem of biblical *hermeneutics*.

In an earlier work, I conducted a brief exercise in hermeneutics on the theme of the exodus.[1] My effort has been well received, especially by those involved in elaborating theology in oppressed countries, and so I decided to broaden and deepen many of its aspects. And I decided to reverse the overall procedure: here, instead of an example of hermeneutic practice with a minimum of theory, I shall set forth a theory of hermeneutics, and take examples of its application from many themes, not only that of the exodus. My earlier exercise, in the hermeneutics of a single theme, was intended precisely to demonstrate, by way of reinterpretation, the development of the meaning of an event as transformed into a kerygmatic matrix. This was an important aspect of the hermeneutic phenomenon. Now, however, I propose to touch on a variety of biblical themes, in order to demonstrate that the hermeneutic phenomenon is omnipresent, and that it expresses an essential trait of the experience of Israel and of the first Christian community.

I shall be inventing nothing. Biblical hermeneutics is simply a method of reading the Bible. But that method must be explicitated and organized. One or another method has always been practiced, of course, but often without explicit awareness of it. The reader will come to see that there is no such thing as a nonhermeneutic reading of the Bible. And this will itself be a great step forward.

Elements of the hermeneutic method must also be organized, so that we may know how to use it and justify it. It is a simple fact that the more the Christian life and therefore theology are—a life and theology that renew—the more they involve a hermeneutics, however implicitly. It is likewise a fact that this renewal is resisted by a traditional practice and a traditional theology. This is a great deal more visible in contexts of cultural, economic, political, and religious domination—which of itself arouses a suspicion as to who is the real addressee of the liberative message proclaimed by the Bible. It is therefore a matter of urgency to acquire the theoretical instrumentation that will enable us to reread the Bible in such a way as to tap its "reservoir of meaning."

For so many Christians, the Bible is more a puzzle than a clear message. Far from our time and place in its origin, with its ancient and often contradictory ideas over the course of its long literary history, with a final text that is frequently difficult to decipher (which is hardly what we look for in a "message")—it is not very attractive in the directioning of our day-to-day lives. Is what it says true? Does it have to "say" anything? Is it God's word? Is it our God or the God of the Hebrews? Many, many questions arise.

Introduction

"Hermeneutics"—literally, "interpretation"—comes from *hermeneuein*, the Greek word for "to interpret." Per se, both words designate the same reality, the first coming to us from Greek and the second from Latin. But the second has entered into common use, and so has diminished in precision. Accordingly, "hermeneutics" is preferred for designating, especially, three aspects of interpretation that must be spelled out.

First and foremost, the "privileged locus" of the hermeneutic function is the interpretation of *texts*. We shall see later what else is implied in this statement. Secondly, it is a matter of common knowledge that all interpreters condition their reading of a text by a kind of *preunderstanding* arising from their own life context. Thirdly—and this is not always well defined, but it will have a central place in my development of the subject of biblical hermeneutics—the interpreter *enlarges* the *meaning* of the text being interpreted.

I hold that any interpretation, whether of texts or events, involves the second and third aspect just mentioned. In my presentation, then, I shall not be concerned to distinguish between hermeneutics and interpretation but neither shall I attempt to reduce them to the texts. Without confusing things we shall see that the interpretation of texts supposes the existence of another process, that of the interpretation of particular practices or events, and that the very constitution of those texts originates in an experience that is *interpreted*. And so I go beyond the limitation imposed by Paul Ricoeur, for example, when he defines hermeneutics as "the *theory* of the functions of *understanding* in their relationship to the *interpretation* of *texts.*"[2] From the hermeneutic viewpoint, text and event or praxis are already mutually conditioned. This is an important observation, precisely in the case of a reading of the Bible, which is done from a point of departure in a practice of faith, with regard to a Bible that signals God's wondrous deeds of salvation. In this one sentence, I have indicated that a reading of the biblical texts is circumscribed by two existential moments, or two historical poles, "sandwiching" the text between them. This enables us to appreciate the "betweenness" of the Bible as a *text*, a text arising from two real-life "vectors."

There is no such thing as a *biblical* hermeneutics distinct from a philosophical, a sociological, a literary hermeneutics, and so on and so on. There is but one general hermeneutics, with many "regional expressions."[3] The method and phenomenon coincide in all cases. It is true, however, that biblical hermeneutics has a rather novel characteristic, in that it takes up texts with a long tradition of elaboration and reelaboration, and originating with a people whose journey was likewise a long one—a people unified by a linear and teleological conceptualization of history. This means that the task of interpretation will be both difficult and fertile. This "hermeneutic fecundity" will stand out clearly throughout my study.

PHILOSOPHICAL HERMENEUTICS: THREE MAJOR PHASES

This is not the place for a history of general hermeneutics, or even of biblical hermeneutics in particular. It will be helpful, however, to point out that there have been three outstanding phases in the "thematization" of hermeneutics. I shall present them in reverse chronological order, in order to show that what seems new is really not terribly so.

1. The Modern Era

In a philosophical context, the problem of hermeneutics is posed by Schleiermacher (ca. 1800), Dilthey (ca. 1900), and later by Heidegger; then by Gadamer and Ricoeur—with celebrated offshoots in the area of theology at the hands of Fuchs, Ebeling, Bultmann, and the post-Bultmannians.

In Schleiermacher and Dilthey, it is interesting to note a great preoccupation with what is *behind* the text—with its history, its author, with *who is expressed* in a text rather than *what* the text says.

Heidegger moves from epistemology to ontology. The "being" he interrogates, *Dasein*, is a *being-in*, a being-in-the-world, a situated being, which, in the act of interpretation, is *pre*understood. Hence, "being-in" the world conditions any interpretation. This militates against any pretension on the part of any subject to be the measure or moderator of objectivity, inasmuch as it pertains to the very essence of a subject to be an "in-habitant" of this world, and this circumscribes the subject. Heidegger sets out for the foundations. But he never returns to epistemology.

Gadamer emphasizes that a human being is within a tradition, and that the act of understanding is a finite occurrence of that tradition, as a way of belonging to history. The historical distance between the text and the interpreter calls for a "fusion of horizons," which is possible because we are dealing with the intrahistorical.

The contribution of Ricoeur—who, for that matter, rereads Heidegger—consists in "closing the circle" of linguistics (looking not only at what lies "behind" a text, but at what lies "in front of" it) in the construction of a fertile theory of hermeneutics.[4]

The post-Heideggerian "theological offshoots" are pre-Ricoeurian, and particularly concerned to assign a special value to the biblical *word* as present "event." (Later I shall turn things around and speak of an *"event become word."*)

These are the milestones in modern reflection on hermeneutics. They have made a remarkable contribution to a philosophical synthesis that has also left its mark on theology.

2. The Middle Ages

During the long medieval tradition, a theological discussion of the *senses* of scripture was commonplace. Along with, or overlaid upon, the literal sense of scripture was a spiritual one, which went by various names—"allegorical," "mystical," "messianic," "christological," and so on. There were disputes on the *four* senses of the Bible: the literal, the allegorical (or christological), the moral (called the "tropological," or "having to do with mores, behavior"), and the eschatological (called the "anagogical, the "leading-up-to"). Countless theories made their appearance. The importance of this fact lies in its basic supposition, which is precisely the hermeneutic supposition: the text of the Old Testament is not exhausted in its primary intention. It says something more.

3. Philo of Alexandria

Another, more ancient, attempt to formalize the hermeneutic problem was made by Philo of Alexandria in the first century B.C. Philo is remarkable not only for his interpretation of Hebrew traditions in a Greek framework, as in his commentary on Genesis, *De Opificio Mundi*, but especially for his effort to penetrate the problem of language.[5]

As I have said, these three stages correspond, respectively, to three attempts to thematize the problem of the interpretation of texts (historical, biblical) or of human existence as such. Of course, not even this is new. The hermeneutic process—unthematized—is constitutive of all tradition, religious and nonreligious. The Bible cannot be understood apart from this process. But it is in the rabbinical tradition of the intertestamentary age that we first discern the overt attempt to read a new meaning beneath the first meaning of the text—a deeper meaning beneath the first meaning of the text—and a deeper meaning behind the simple meaning of the words, by the processes of *darash* and *pashat* (in the Aramaic terminology of the time).[6] This question will come up again later, when targum and midrash are discussed.

This historical sketch will have prepared us for a consideration of hermeneutics from a directly biblical perspective.

FIVE APPROACHES TO THE BIBLE

The Bible has come under different focuses, all of them orientated to the exploration of its meaning or message. Some approaches explore the "problem" of a current reading of the Bible; others try to penetrate the biblical content. Let us look at five general approaches.

1. Present Reality as Primary "Text"

The Bible can be relegated to a secondary level, as a "de-actualized" text, a text no longer speaking to the present, and contrasted with present reality as a "text" and understood as the prime *locus theologicus* for the discovery of a God speaking to and calling on human beings. This reality is conceived of as so charged with meaning that any other theological "signifier" is thought of as secondary. When options are clear, there is no reason to appeal to the Bible.

Is this not the attitude of a great number of Christians committed to revolutionary struggle against the unjust structures of the socio-economic system they are living in? They ask: Does the gospel say anything *new* to us? The question is a sincere one but, I believe, it reflects a methodological flaw, emerging from a traditional reading of the Bible that has alienated it from the real history of men and women. This obstacle can be detected in the work of certain liberation theologians who are more attentive than others to socio-historical praxis as a parameter of theological reflection.

2. Concordism

Another route consists in taking the Bible as it is, and seeking "correspondences" between real-life situations and occurrences related in the scriptures. When such a correspondence is found, God is considered to be speaking through the "archetypal event."

Even at first glance, this approach to the Bible is "concordistic." Concordism—so widespread, especially in fundamentalistic readings of the sacred text—has two negative qualities. First, it limits the biblical message to situations having a parallel in the history of Israel or of the first Christian communities, as if God were incapable of self-revelation in any other manner. It is an instance of theological reductionism. Secondly, concordism superficializes the biblical message, restricting it to the level of external fact, and confusing *what happens* with the *meaning* of what happens.

The same danger can be seen when, in some theologies, *continuity* is sought between the ideas of the Old or New Testament and those of a given culture—Asian, African, or Latin American. But what, then, when such cultural identifications are not to be had—for example, between Hebrew and Greek anthropology? For the Greeks, God was practically "unrevealable"! And yet today there is so much interest in seeking out similarities between African or pre-Columbian traditions and the Hebrew *Weltanschauung*. Kerygma becomes confused with its cultural garb, with its "contextualization."

It is true that the search for "resonances" between the Bible and a contemporary (cultural, and especially socio-historical) context can be a point of departure for exploring the pertinency of the Bible for women and men of today. What is really impoverishing in concordism comes to the fore when the "resonances" discovered are historical or scientific, and confirmation of the content of the Bible is found in certain data of modern science (such as geological eras seen as corresponding to the "days" in the Genesis account of the creation of the world), or in pairing historical "facts" in the Bible with non-biblical facts or events. In the former case, there is no real confirmation. In both cases, the sacred text is emptied of its kerygmatic content, and any hermeneutic effort of investigation of a deeper meaning of the text becomes superfluous. And yet the concordistic reading of the Bible has been so widespread, even in the area of systematic theology!

3. Historico-Critical Methods

The exegetical methods formulated by modern biblical criticism have blazed new trails for an approach to the Bible. Today we are able to go back to the historical and cultural milieu in which a scriptural passage took shape, and we have a better contextualization of its original meaning. Critical exegesis has broken with naive "historicist" and concordistic readings of the Bible, which, as we have just seen, prevent us from getting to the real meaning of a text. But more than this, it has significantly broadened the exploration of texts. Literary criticism, of "forms" and of literary genres or codes, of oral and literary traditions, of redaction, has revolutionized biblical studies in recent decades, correcting many defects in Christian theology, and indirectly promoting renewal in all areas of theological activity.

Alongside these indisputable benefits, which render these methods indispensable and priceless, their exaggerated, indeed at times reductionistic, use does entail certain risks. For one thing, they bring out the "behind," the archeology, of a text, very strongly, and thereby shift the attention of the exegete or Bible reader to a precanonical level. For example, the Pentateuch can now be interpreted in accordance with the

√Priestly

Yahwist, Elohist, Deuteronomist, /sacerdotal, and other sources. Emphasis falls on the *pre*-text. Literary criticism enables us to identify the traces of the formation of a work, or part of a work; other methods lead us to its remote origins, and then back to its present state via the history of its redaction. This vast arc, from the text to its first beginnings and back again, is a *history* of the text rather than an exploration of its meaning—unless its meaning is identified with the meaning of the earlier strata, when these are accessible to us.

But the meaning of the Pentateuch cannot be understood only on the basis of the Yahwist and other sources. In the first place, we do not know how much of this work has been included in the Pentateuch redaction. Besides, the author of the Pentateuch has composed a new work, whose meaning is not in the fragments used, but in the structured totality of the new whole. Redaction criticism mitigates this defect somewhat; but in speaking of the "redactor" instead of the "author," and in calling itself "redaction *history*," it places the emphasis on the formation of the text rather than on the text itself.

Then again, a concern with legitimating the noetic sciences, so peculiar to Western mentality over the last several centuries, has concentrated attention on the literal meaning of the Bible, understood as the "historical" meaning (as is shown by the very name, "*historico*-critical methods").[7] This, too, is a form of reductionism.[8] Hence the interest in the intention of the "redactor" of such and such a text, contextualized by the use of all possible resources. This is important, provided the text in question not be evacuated of all its meaning by an attempt to make its meaning reside ultimately in the preredaction, as I have said. But furthermore, in clinging to the *intention of the author or redactor* as the sole meaning, we run the risk of shutting up the message of the Bible in the past, and the Bible becomes a "deposit" of a "definitive meaning," coincident with the thought of the redactor, or even of the preredactors, of the text as we have it. I do not think that the significative possibilities of a text end here. For a theology of oppressed peoples, especially, this approach offers only a partial solution. Its importance is undeniable. One must pass this way. But one must not rest here.

4. Structural Analysis

A more recent contribution to biblical studies is forthcoming from the sciences of language, especially linguistics and narrative semiotics. The sciences of language and literature have always made a positive contribution to our knowledge of the Bible. But the recent development of *structural* analysis is being applied to biblical texts with good results. The study of the underlying structure—narrative (agents and functions) as well as discursive (thematic roles, axes of meaning)—is a help for "centering" the meaning of a text. The surface structure, on the other hand, commonly called simply the "literary structure," is even more fertile, inasmuch as it gives us certain reading keys emerging from the codification of a text. Enriching as it is, however, this method is only a point of departure in the quest for meaning. Below we shall see how helpful it is. But in itself it is reductionistic, insofar as it abstracts from the "life" of a text—its history, its cultural, social, or religious milieu.

5. Hermeneutics

The fifth approach to the biblical kerygma is that of hermeneutics—what this book is all about. Let us begin with some preliminary observations. I have alluded above to the difference between "interpretation" and "hermeneutics." I do not regard as adequate the Bultmannian notion of hermeneutics, nor that of Fuchs, Ebeling, or their successors.[9] Yes, there is a *pre*understanding, a *Voverständnis*, in the reading of the Bible. This is a fact, and it is of the highest value for our purposes. Yes, the Bible is a "language event," a *Sprache-*

reignis, or a "word event," a *Wortereignis*, in all its concreteness, but this does not exhaust the Bible, nor is it sufficient. Exclusive attention to this formality fails to explicitate the objective conditions of the Bible as *language*. It gives the original referent of a text short shrift, and encourages an individualistic reading of the Bible.[10]

In order to understand hermeneutics in all its wealth and methodological value, then, it will behoove us to approach it by way of the sciences of language. Hermeneutics deals with the interpretation of texts—or of events gathered up in language. It will therefore be imperative to situate hermeneutics first of all on the foundation of semiotics, the science of signs, whose most comprehensive expression is that of language in the strict sense. Another point of contact is rooted in the fact that hermeneutics and semiotics both have to do with reading as a production (not repetition) of meaning.

At first blush, we are faced with a paradox. Hermeneutics seems to be connected with diachrony, with the becoming of meaning—with the semantics or transformation of the meaning of words or texts. By contrast, semiotics prioritizes synchrony—simultaneity—and the structural laws governing the effectuation of language. But I speak of approaching hermeneutics "by way of" semiotics—not of confusing it or identifying it with semiotics. True, the focuses are diametrically opposite. But they are not contradictory. They converge. Returning from semiotics to hermeneutics, in respect for the individuality of each, the latter is now solidly founded, solidly based. Let us take this lengthy route, then. At its conclusion, we shall find biblical hermeneutics supplied with a good deal more light.

I conclude this Introduction with a summary of the focuses or approaches to the biblical text (as to any other literary work) in Diagram 1. As it indicates, a text can be contemplated from various angles—studied by different methods, which are not mutually exclusive but which ought to converge, for a better understanding of the work in question (in our case, the Bible). The only approach not appearing here is the concordist, because it does not lead to meaning but away from it.

Diagram 1
Approaches to a (Biblical) Text

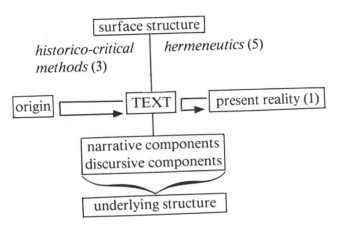

Historico-critical methods: from the text to its origin, and back to the text.

Hermeneutics: not only from present reality (1), but from it to the text, and back to present reality.

NB: *Numerals refer to the numbered sections in the Introduction; note the omission of 2.*

1

From Semiotics to Hermeneutics

Our concern is with hermeneutics. But, as I have already stated, hermeneutics must fall partly within the vast field of the science of *signs*. Human texts and events are signs that call for interpretation. This is not the place for an *ex professo* examination of linguistics or semiotics. It will be sufficient to point out a few facts of language that will help to explain the hermeneutic phenomenon.

LANGUAGE AS SYSTEM AND AS EVENT

It is customary in linguistics to make a distinction between "language" *(lengua, langue)* and "speech" *(habla, parole)*. The former is the systems of signs and laws regulating grammar and syntax—a sort of "canon" establishing guidelines for meaning. It is based on structure, which supposes differences, oppositions, and closed relationships within a given language, functioning synchronically, but more on the unconscious than on the reflexive level. The repertory of linguistic signs in a given language is finite and closed. There is a limit to the number of combinations that can be made. And there is an underlying potential polysemy. "Volume," for example, can make you think of a book, or of a geometrical measure of

13

capacity. "Chestnut" is a tree, but it is also a color. All languages have an abundance of polysemous words.

Furthermore, even "monosemous" (univocal) words—the majority—mean nothing as they stand in the dictionary. Indeed, a sentence with a linguistic meaning (i.e., having a relationship between the signifier—the sign, the word—and the significate—the content) can be ambiguous, in virtue of an extralinguistic referent. "Jesus Christ saves us" is a correct sentence—it has a grammatical and an existential meaning— but it is equivocal in its reference. From what does he save us? When? And so on. Something else is needed to "close" the meaning in a precise direction. This is language as "competency," as specialists in linguistics say.

But now this system of signs, this language, must be "activated," by having it *used* to *say something about something.* Now we are in the moment of "speech," the "event" of a language. Speech is the *act* executing the given possibilities residing within a system of signs. Three factors contribute to the "closure of meaning" in a single direction.

1) First there is the *sender,* or speaker, who selects the signs (words, sentences, codes, or literary genres possible in a given language) to transmit the message. The signs set up a mutual relationship, forming a structure. It is basic, then, to identify this structure in order to decode a message. Hence the importance of all structural analysis, in biblical exegesis as in the exegesis of any text.

2) Then there is the *receiver,* or concrete interlocutor, to whom the message, coded in a determinate way, is addressed, and who is able to decipher it—an instantaneous operation that is one of the marvels of human language.

3) Finally, there is a *context,* or horizon of understanding, common to the sender and the receiver, enabling them to "coincide" in the reference or denotation of the message— that on which the message bears. Without this common milieu—linguistic, cultural, social, geographical, and so on, or as many other dimensions as human reality may be

said to have—language remains polysemous.

In the act of discourse—in the "speech act"—there must be a *closure* of the potential polysemy residing in the words or sentences. Otherwise it is impossible to communicate—unless a deliberate polysemy is intended, as in poetry or symbolic language, and even in this case the context (at all events, the dialogue between the interlocutors) helps "close" the meaning of a word or statement. Otherwise, discourse is no longer a "saying something about something," which, after all, is the intent of the one who speaks, writes a letter to a friend, or recounts a story to an audience.

In the "speech event," the receiver of the message exercises a process of assimilation or grasp of the linguistic code selected by the sender for the act of communication. As in music, so also in language, the message comes in a "key," or code, which the hearer grasps directly and immediately. To confuse codes would be to sidetrack the direction of the message altogether. Just as it is necessary to tune a radio to a given wavelength, so also must one "be in tune" when it comes to language.

I shall return to this matter when I deal with the hermeneutic process properly so-called. For now, I note only that the traditional reading of the Bible is found wanting here, and on an essential point: all texts are interpreted in a *historical* "key." In no other body of literature have such elementary mistakes been committed. It is as if one heard all musical compositions in a single key! This only highlights the importance of the sciences of language—especially that of "narrative semiotics," as we shall see—for validating one's understanding of biblical texts.

LANGUAGE AS TEXT AND AS WRITING

Between language and speech, between competency and its actualization (or "performance," the gallicism used in linguistics), between system and use, a first *distantiation* takes place, whose badge is the "closure" of meaning. No temporal or spatial distance is involved, of course; the "distance" is of the logical order.

Language, however, is not exhausted in this step. A new distantiation, which I shall call a "second distantiation," now occurs. The second distantiation is produced when discourse crystalizes in a transmitted "text." I use this term in a broad sense. A "text" can be either written or oral. A myth, for example, or a song, may well be passed from generation to generation orally before becoming fixed in writing. Nearly all the biblical narratives began as oral traditions in some form. And they were already "texts." A text is a "texture," etymologically, a web, in which the elements of language (words, sentences, literary units, and other elements) are organized according to structural functions that *as such* produce a meaning.

The laws of the linguistics of the sentence are repeated and broadened on the level of the account. There is actually a grammar and a syntax of the account.[11] Here again structure is important, with its "differences" and relationships, and with its character as an organized totality.

A text is something structured and finished. It has limits and internal relationships. This characteristic of a text has consequences that call for our attention. The first is the capacity of a text to bestow meaning in virtue of what it is— the *coding* of a message. Secondly, the oral or written text is open to a new understanding thanks to the second distantiation, that between "speech" or the act of discourse and the inscription of meaning in such or such a text. This distancing takes place in the three factors that have previously contributed to the closure of meaning, and now contribute to its opening. Let me list and explain these factors in the same order:

1) The original *sender* disappears in a text. Authors (if we are speaking of writing) "die" in the very act of coding their message. The inscription of meaning in any account or text is a

creative act in which one lays down one's life, figuratively speaking. A correct understanding of this phenomenon is important for that hermeneutics which uses linguistics and invalidates the attempts of older formulations (e.g., that of Schleiermacher) as well as the attempts of historico-critical methods to recover and revive the *author* of a text.

2) Nor is the first *"receiver"* or interlocutor present. The one reading a written text, or hearing a traditional account—a myth or a biblical passage—is not its first addressee. This change of addressees of a message is much more important in the case of religious texts, mythical or not, which claim ongoing meaning and validity for centuries, generation after generation.

3) For the same reason, the *horizon* of the original discourse disappears; the cultural and historical context is no longer the same; current addressees receiving the message have another "world" of interests, concerns, culture, and so on.

These three aspects (much emphasized by Paul Ricoeur in his later hermeneutical works), taken together, help us understand the hermeneutic process.[12] The *author,* as someone "speaking," disappears and can no longer be interviewed for the meaning of what he or she has "said." Henceforth the narrator is not a person of flesh and blood, but a linguistic presence. There is someone narrating or writing, but we can recognize that person *only in the text*. This physical absence, however, is semantic wealth. The closure of meaning imposed by the speaker is now transformed into an openness of meaning. Now the narrator is the text itself, not someone coming in from the outside, of whom explanations can be sought. This concentration in the text makes it possible to explore the possible meanings of the text *as text*.

Next, the appearance of a new *receiver,* likewise situated on a new horizon of understanding, removes the text still further from its original framework, and from contact with its author. When persons speak, they transmit a message (in locutional language, as has been said) with a particular emphasis or intensity (and this is *in*locutional language, expressed by intonation, gestures, and so on), and with an effect that is part of the message (*per*locutional language).[13] In the reading of a text, the last-named two languages or nuances are lost, to the extent that they are less "inscribable" in a code, inlocution disappearing more, perlocution less.

The reception of the message of the text is not the same, then, for the receiver who hears the message as its first addressee and for the receiver who reads it as its second addressee. For that matter, even if the text were to be a tape recording, listening to it would not be a simple repetition of the act of hearing it "live"; at least the context would no longer be the same, and the text would produce other meaning-effects. Similarly, when we hear a text being read aloud the *text* is the speaker; the person reading it aloud is just another addressee! But the reader, not the writer, does the speaking; the writer can no longer speak. And yet the writer's presence is as apparent but unreal as that the sun revolves around the earth. Again, we come back to the *autonomy* of the text, which will condition the hermeneutic openness of the act of reading.

And then what happens? The author's finite horizon is replaced by a textual infinitude. The account opens up again to a polysemy, and not only a *potential* polysemy, as on the level of "language," but a *potentiated* polysemy, made possible by the network of significates or meanings that constitute a work. This textual openness awaits new addressees, with their own "world."

It is easy to understand that a letter of Paul to particular addressees—Colossians, Romans, or the like—where the author and his readers confront a specific problem, had to change perspective when it was universalized in the primitive church. The new receivers of the text were not delimited by the previous reading made by the Christians of a particular time and place, nor could they ask Paul what he meant by this or that sentence.

Any text is open to many readings, none of which repeats another. The greater the distance from the author, the greater the dimensions acquired by the rereading of a text. Conversely, the greater the semantic wealth of an account, the further removed its author is from the mind of the interpreter.

This is why sacred texts or mythic accounts are usually anonymous—not only because they are sometimes the progressive creation of a community, but, more importantly, because they have their meaning by virtue of what they say rather than by virtue of the one who says it. It seems that their depth of meaning is more profound the less that is known about the authors. Thus in the case of the Bible we know nothing about the individual identity of any of the authors of the Old Testament, and only very little about the authors of the New.[14]

Instead, it is typical of religious texts (but not they alone) to be attributed to some later, prominent figure—the Psalms are attributed to David, the Pentateuch to Moses, the wisdom literature to Solomon, certain New Testament letters to Paul, and so on, once the later figure is *already* important—for whatever reason. This hermeneutic phenomenon will become clearer in the course of this study.

Another facet of the same phenomenon is the physical expansion of an author's text by successive rereadings, without any modification in the traditional attribution of authorship. This is the case with the Gospel of Matthew, as with other writings of the New Testament. Matthew is the author of a primitive Aramaic nucleus; the present form of the Gospel is the result of subsequent reworking. But tradition continues to call it the *text* of Matthew.

Key elements of this section are summed up in Diagram 2 (see page 20).

Diagram 2
Distantiation 1 and 2

Language	*Speech*	*Text/Writing*
Phonemes/ Terms	Sentence	Account
System	Use/"Event"	Narrative codes/ Structure
Finite, closed repertory	Infinite repertory	
Naming	Saying something about something to someone	Saying something about something to an infinitude of readers
Atemporal	Transitory	Permanent
Polysemy	*Closure*	*Polysemy*

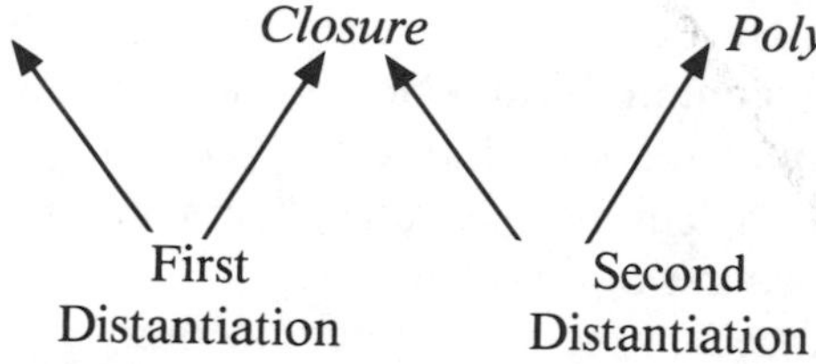

First Distantiation   Second Distantiation

READING AS PRODUCTION OF MEANING: THE HERMENEUTIC ACT

It is said in semiotics that meaning is not something "objective" and palpable in a text, as in a pure state. Otherwise exegetes could *find* meaning, thanks to their technical ability, and philological and historical resources. It would only be a matter of good fortune to discover *the* meaning of a text. In the case of a text given a number of interpretations, all but one would be mistaken. The decision as to which one was the true one would come from an extratextual "authority."

In the final analysis, this view of things supposes that "the" meaning of a text coincides with the author's intention, and that a later reader must repeat the reading made by the first addressees. And we are caught in the snare of exegetical "historicism." Worse, the message is atrophied and cannot unfold into new, creative readings. It may even cease to be a message.

But the process of reinterpretation is so compelling that attempts to "fix" the meaning of a biblical text have ended up in formulas that, in time, have had to be reread. This shows that the attempt to lock up *the* meaning of a text is futile and unreal.

Indeed, any reading is the *production* of discourse, and thus of a meaning, from a point of departure in a text. We do not read a meaning but a text, an account, actualizing its *competency,* competency which is analyzed by semiotics. In this way, a text is open to various patterns. The structural analysis of an account or discourse is not endowed with the precision one finds in mathematics; results vary according to different combinations of elements. The structure of an *account* is analyzed in terms of its "narrative program"—the actantial figures in the text; the "functions" of the text. The structure of a *discourse* is analyzed in terms of semantic axes, semiotic framework, verification, and so on, as the piecing together of *one* among many possible meanings of words or themes within a given society or worldview.[15] In either case, different results emerge from different combinations. It may even happen that the language contains so many elements of meaning that no analysis can exhaust the possible combinations and thus reveal the total meaningfulness.

The plurality of readings suggested by semiotic practice is not due to the ambiguity of a text, but to its capacity to say many things at once.[16] And structural analysis is not interpretation of a text. It only prepares for it.

On the properly interpretive level, various readings take

place, made by different disciplines. One and the same text can be given a phenomenological reading, a historical reading, a sociological, psychological, literary, theological reading, and so on. Each of these readings of one and the same account is the *production of a discourse* from a point of departure in this text. It is a *text on a text,* a text about a text. A plurality is possible because the discourse calls into play a plurality of codes, which each reading selects and organizes. Furthermore, the readings practiced at the various levels are not the exclusive readings of *one* interpreter discovering *the* meaning of the text. Each reading is a production of meaning, and, as we know, authors "die," leaving their text to its own keeping, and now the text, as a coded structure, is inscribed by a moment of production and a moment of reading and interpretation. In other words it becomes polysemic, even from the viewpoint of semiotics alone. It holds various possibilities of meaning, which emerge when it is read according to any of the codes from among its store. Persons who are experienced in the reading of texts are aware of this phenomenon.

I shall complete these observations by exemplifying them in a biblical passage. Let us take, for instance, John 1:35–51, the call of the first disciples. How much has been written of this passage in exegetical commentaries! What inspiration the Christian practice of Jesus' discipleship has drawn from them! One can return to this text time and time again and still produce meaning. One way of doing so consists in identifying the different codes that intersect in this pericope. Let us take the account in its present form and isolate the thematic roles as they come on the scene. "The next day" connects this narrative with the foregoing one—the one beginning with verse 29, whose own "the next day" connects it with the narrative beginning with verse 19 (itself containing a "when"). In verse 43 we again read "the next day," to be completed by the "on the third day" of 2:1. This chronological code, which may appear stodgy or artificial, is actually weaving a theology— that of the first day of the *new creation,* in which the Logos is preexistent (John 1:1) as the Word of the creation of the world (Gen. 1:1 in the targum rereading). Of course, the theme of the new creation is not stated in a *formula;* it is "stated" by the structure of the account—which structure, in turn, combines with the other reading codes of the same text to yield a mutual conferral of meaning.

There follows a scene of human encounters. First, John stands with two of his disciples (v. 35b); all of them come upon Jesus (v. 39). Then one of the disciples, Andrew, "seek[s] out" his brother Simon (v. 41a), and testifies to him, "We have *found* the Messiah!" (v. 41b). A new series of encounters begins in verse 43: Jesus meets Philip, then Philip meets Nathanael, and tells him, "We have *found* the one Moses spoke of . . ." (v. 45). The word "found" in each series means "encountered" in both a physical and a spiritual sense, with emphasis on the latter, in the sense of "recognizing," "acknowledging" (the Messiah, "the one Moses spoke of")—an "encounter" that is possible only on a higher level.

Other codes show the same shift of levels: in "seeing," for example, from the ocular level (vv. 36, 38, 39 [twice], 42, 46, 47, 50) to another, deeper level (vv. 48, 50 ["You will *see* much greater things . . ."]), and finally to a theophanic "seeing" (v. 51). Obviously this motif connects with the acceptance of the *signs* in following sequences (see 2:11 and the other miracle accounts). The signs are indeed "seen." This Johannine "seeing" is a reference to faith, and not just to "seeing" with one's eyes (v. 50 and John 20:29).[17] The incarnation of the Word mediates faith realities through human realities. This is why the theme of faith in the One Sent has so much relevance in John.

Likewise apparent in this account is the onomastic code. Proper names abound. Jesus' name occurs ten times, and he is identified as the "son of Joseph, the one from Nazareth" (v. 45). Giving titles to persons is a prevalent motif of the fourth Gospel, and the titles given have a theological value. And so we have an onomastic code, a code of identification, which is probably the most important one in our text at hand. Jesus is the "lamb of God" (v. 36), "Rabbi, (which means Teacher)" (v. 38—the Hebrew word *rabbi* is given even in the Greek text, to ensure a connection with the Jewish magisterial tradition, and avoid confusion with the Greek *didaskalos),* "Messiah" (v. 41), "the one Moses spoke of in the law—the prophets too" (v. 45), "Son of God . . . king of Israel" (v. 49), the "Son of Man" (v. 51).

The list of names is important simply as a list, of course, in preparation for subsequent passages. But there is more to it than this. The names are distributed in precise places. They open and close the total account of verses 35–51. Each series marked by the temporal reference "the next day" (vv. 35–42, 43–51) contains three titles for Jesus and one more for someone else: Simon is Simon "Peter the Rock" in the former, and Nathanael is the "true Israelite" in the latter (vv. 41–47). In the second series, Jesus' identification as the "meaning" of the Old Testament, and Nathanael's identification as the "true Israelite"—an evident reference to the "meaning" of Israel— counterbalance each other.

Finally, there is the "movement" code (going, coming, following: vv. 37, 38, 39, 40, 43, 46), which suggests the *following* of Jesus, and which in turn is set in semantic counterpoint, but theological complementarity, with the "lodging" and "staying" of verse 39—which, on another level, prepares for the *menein* in Jesus, the "abiding in Jesus," that is so typically Johannine.

We could go on and on with this so well woven, or textured, account, in terms of still different codes. How pregnant with meaning it is in the light of semiotics! The adventure of reading a text as an inexhaustible production of meaning, and therefore as continual re-creation of the message, is easier to appreciate now. Later on, I shall examine other approaches to the exploration of the message of a text, approaches equally reinforced by the contribution of semiotics.

IMPLICATIONS OF READING AS PRODUCTION OF MEANING

There are, in the relationship between semiotics and hermeneutics, between the force of the text and the "force" of life, certain effects and certain demands that it will be helpful to examine in order to come to a better awareness of the scope of an interpretive reading of biblical texts.

Transformation and Its Concealment

In every text, there is a "forward"—the world of meanings that opens up in virtue of the textual polysemy "potentiated" by the very condition of the text as linguistic structure, and in virtue of the "death" of its author, as we have seen. The meaning is now in the text, not in the mind of its author. But it is not in the text as a separable entity; rather it is "coded" in a system of signs constituting the account and "saying something about something" by virtue of its manifestation as *this* discourse.

This summarizes a good many of the foregoing points. Now it is time to explain to what extent each reading of a "speaking" text transforms *what* it says and that *about which* it speaks, while concealing this transformation. I shall utilize the accounts of the so-called Servant of Yahweh songs of Second Isaiah: Isaiah 42:1–7; 49:1–9a; 50:4–11; 52:13–53:12.

Supposing the original independence of these songs vis-à-vis the rest of Isaiah 40–55 (Deutero-Isaiah), and supposing they were composed before the formation of the "book" of Isaiah as we have it today (Isa. 1–66), we see that they present a personage of royal characteristics who receives the mission from God to deliver the people of Israel, captive among gentiles. He is persecuted, humiliated, and put to death, but finally exalted. His suffering is vicarious, inasmuch as "it was our infirmities that he bore, our sufferings that he endured"

(Isa. 53:4); he was "smitten for the sin of his people" (53:8); "he bore the sins of many, and won pardon for their offenses" (53:12). The discourse here is the vehicle of a meaning emerging from the organization of in-depth codes (involving actants and functions) and surface codes (in symbols, stylistic devices, literary genre, and so on). The text yields a meaning in virtue of the position of linguistic *signifiers* referring to *significates* that remain within the account, *even though* we have lost the identity of their *extralinguistic* referent (Joakim? Zerubbabel? Israel itself? A prophet? A sage?).[18]

The critical methods of biblical exegesis are a help to us in the identification of a possible referent for these songs. But this is not where the reading key is. This is only an attempt to recover the "behind" of the text, the life situation that originated it as a first production of meaning. Important as the "historical" reading of these texts is, stopping there would mean falling victim to a risk that must be avoided. It would mean attempting to reduce the meaning of the text to its first production, which would imply the exhaustion of the text at the very moment that it begins to demonstrate its polysemy. And gravest of all, it would mean binding ourselves to a kind of "historicism," from which will then arise the exegetical concordisms that, on the naive pretext of sorting out the relevance of God's word for the present, immobilize it in its first reference. In this way, approaches as contrary as critical exegesis and concordism converge, as they attempt simply to crystalize the meaning of texts. And priority is finally assigned to the referent—an extralinguistic factor—over the meaning and import of the text itself. But *rereadings flow from the text, not from the referent.* This is an important principle, which has recently brought semiotics even closer to hermeneutics. The referent of a text is a closure of meaning from the very moment of the production of that meaning. A text, like any language-in-act, can communicate a meaning only by a form of closure, which delivers the extralinguistic referent— that to which the text refers in order to say something to someone. By contrast, the text itself, as structuration of signifiers and significates that generate meaning, is polysemous, and entails a very strong tendency *not* to retain the historical referent especially in religious texts or others that are reinterpreted time and again. This referent is ballast, to be jettisoned.

It seems to me that this is precisely the case with the songs of the Deutero-Isian "Servant." Why has the historical personage to whom they referred once upon a time not been retained? Why must we identify him, by recourse to so many celebrated hypotheses, in order to understand the message of these magnificent accounts—hypotheses that may send us back to a preredactional stage that is simply not at the level of the current kerygmatic texts? Knowing whether the figure of the "Servant" is Joakim or someone else would clarify the *genesis* of the text, but not the *text*. We are in danger of committing an error of perspective.

The very fact that the songs in question do not explicitly indicate their referent leaves their interpretation more open. The poetic, symbolic expression orientates them in the same direction. But these considerations do not constitute the sole conditions of the polysemy residing in the text. They favor it. But the accounts are polysemous in their very linguistic structure. And so they project "forward," calling for the manifestation of a "surplus of meaning." Thus their reading will be a *production* of meaning, not a repetition of the first meaning. This is basic for an understanding of the hermeneutic process. No wonder, then, that these songs have been reread, by successive generations, in so many different ways. I can distinguish four stages in the history of this rereading.

1) The canonical recension—the redaction, the wording, in which the Servant songs were admitted to the received catalogue of sacred books—itself shows signs of an updating of the referent as a means of closing the meaning of the poems. In Isaiah 49:3, the Hebrew text that has come down to us identifies the Servant with Israel ("You are my servant . . .

Israel"), apparently with no regard for internal contradiction with verses 5–6, which speak of the Servant as *sent to* Israel. For literary criticism, this is an "inconsistent gloss." Hermeneutically, this gloss is rich, as a transfer of meaning to an updated referent in virtue of the needs of the community that is handing down the text.

2) In the Septuagint, the collective interpretation predominates. The songs refer again and again to the persecuted Israel of the diaspora, emphasizing its salvific mission.[19]

3) The New Testament resumes the individual interpretation favored by the symbolism of the texts, which speak of one person. (This does not mean, let me repeat, that the reference is to an individual.) Thus the shift to a christological reading was facilitated. This reading was so powerful, in light of Christian experience, that it permeates many pages of the New Testament.[20]

4) The Targum of Jonathan (second century A.D.) resumes the collective exegesis (the Servant as Israel) for Isaiah 49:7, applies 42:1–9 to the Messiah and 50:4–11 to the prophet Isaiah, and avoids any allusion at all to the Messiah in the fourth song (Isa. 52:13–53:12).

How were so many rereadings of a single text possible, unless it was actually open somehow? By the same token, we too can reread it without being limited by the christological reading of the New Testament. Paul himself had already extended the figure of the Servant as "light of the gentiles" to himself (Gal. 1:15; in one of the Lukan accounts of Paul's vocation, Acts 26:18; and in the episode of Antioch, Acts 13:47). Today, too, situations exist in which persons, groups of persons, or whole peoples call for a new interpretation of these songs—these mighty compendia of the presence of God and of the trust of those working in God's service. None of these readings of the Deutero-Isaian text are conditioned by the first reference of the account, a reference that is now lost once and for all. They are conditioned only *by the text itself,* in virtue of its coded literary polysemy.

Textual Dependency

Every textual interpretation has to begin with *the text*. It cannot be an arbitrary, hit-or-miss "commentary." It must strive to be a reading of the received *text*. When the risen Jesus reproaches the disciples on the road to Emmaus ("What little sense you have! How slow you are to believe all that *the prophets* have announced! Did not the Messiah *have* to undergo all this so as to enter into his glory?"—Luke 24:25–26) he refers to a *text*, which he says he is interpreting. Now, there is no prophetical text in the Old Testament having the messianic referent that Jesus says according to Luke. Actually, Jesus is clearly alluding to the Servant songs of Isaiah 40–55. (See also Luke 24:46: "Thus it is written that the Messiah must suffer and rise from the dead on the third day.") It seems unlikely that Luke is echoing the rabbinical tradition of a certain messiah, the son of a Joseph, an Ephraimite who, according to certain rabbinical texts, was to suffer.[21] The Lukan dependence on the *Davidic* messianic traditions is clear (Jesus' birth in Bethlehem; the references to David in Luke 1:32, 69; 3:31; and 20:41–44; the theology of Jerusalem). Moreover, the Ephraimite hypothesis is unnecessary. Rather, the Lukan citation demonstrates a linkage to the prophetical text that is the reversible effect both of the linguistic phenomenon of polysemy (see the previous section) and of the "textual" dependency of the hermeneutic act. The rereading becomes "text." The rereading of Isaiah 53 made by the Jesus of Luke 24 is a production of meaning. And it is expressed as a discourse on another, earlier discourse, which it represents itself as subsuming. In perspective, only one discourse, only one text, appears.

The Greek Septuagint text of the Servant songs is not a literal translation of the original Hebrew, but an adaptation, regardless of which recension was used. The reason for this was surely not an ignorance of the Hebrew language. Then why did the translators not translate literally, and make their interpretation in a fresh account instead? Impossible. Their reading originates *in the text* of Isaiah (and never as a parallel interpretation)—and it must express *this* text, the one consecrated by tradition. Accordingly, the text of the Septuagint is a discourse (in the semiotic sense of the word) on another discourse (the text of Isaiah), but presenting both as a single discourse (the text *of Isaiah).*

For the same reason, the interpretation placed by Luke in the mouth of Jesus also refers to the *text* of Isaiah 53. In the targumic version of this poem, on the other hand, there are so many discrepancies with respect to the Hebrew that the text is more like a midrash. A comparison of the Hebrew text with the Aramaic reveals that as much as 50 percent of the Aramaic fails to correspond to the Hebrew.[22] Nevertheless, it must be pointed out that the text thus presented is considered by the rabbinical tradition to be the text *of Isaiah.* It is not the historical personage of Isaiah that is of interest, but the canonical *text,* handed down by tradition and held to be the "word of God."

Hence the supreme importance of any reading as a *reading of a text.* This phenomenon—and now we are at the heart of hermeneutics—does no more than set in relief two things that I have already repeatedly stated: (1) any text is the concentration of a polysemy that opens it "to the fore," in virtue of its condition as a structural "texture" of linguistic codes; (2) any reading of a text is a production of meaning in new codes, which in turn generate other readings as production of meaning, and so on. Interpretation is a chain process, and not repetitive, but ascending. The text contains a reservoir of meaning, ever exploited and never exhausted.

Appropriation of Meaning

From another point of view, reading as production of meaning can also mean an appropriation of meaning. A kind of dependency is established with respect to the text interpreted, and a need arises to possess *all* its meaning. This phenomenon does tremendous violence in the reading of texts that have a great impact on praxis, such as religious, political, or ideological texts. The pretension to meaning is totalitarian and exclusive. It is never shared. It is an "appropriation," exactly. It can leave no gaps for other readings to fill in. In the very act of implicitly depending on an inexhaustible reservoir of meaning in the text, which permits its rereading, the interpreter attempts to "exhaust" it, leaving nothing to another reading.

Hence the "conflict of interpretations." Inasmuch as each interpretation holds itself to be *the* interpretation, it accepts no other. And strife is born. This is the typical phenomenon emerging from the great texts that have inspired historical movements and given rise to groups with their own *Weltanschauung*.

We have examples in the texts of Marx, the Bible, and Hindu tradition. Doctrines very disparate are gathered into the sacred books of the Vedas in India. It is very revealing that Vedanta, a philosophical speculation that all but ceased to echo the religious teaching of the Vedas, today, at a distance of more than two thousand years, is presented as their interpretation. Its very name—*vedanta,* "end of the Vedas"—connotes the claim to exhaust the meaning of the Vedas.

Marx's texts are eloquent in the matter of the interpretive, ideological, and political struggle that they continue to feed. But each Marxist current, in its own evaluation, holds itself out as *the* reading of the great texts of Marx. I cite this case, which has nothing to do with religion, as evidence that linkage to a text of the past is not a peculiarity of the religious worldview. It is to be found even in a socio-political praxis that claims to deny the possibility of any source of knowledge but praxis.

Now let us return to the songs of the Servant of Yahweh of Second Isaiah. The readings done by the writers of the Septuagint, the Essenes of the Dead Sea (in the Qumran scrolls), the primitive church (in the New Testament), and the Targum of

Isaiah 53 were not "possible" readings for their respective groups. They were *the* sense of the prophetical text. This totalitarian aspect of exegesis is more visible, for example, in the targumic interpretation, where an anti-Christian polemic is recognizable—an attempt to block the Christian reading of these so pregnant texts. Thus the translation of the Isaian text into the Aramaic vernacular of the time, with the technical name "targum," swept aside any possible reference in Isaiah 53 to the suffering of an individual messiah, thus attempting to invalidate an exegesis already carried out by Christians with the person of Jesus of Nazareth in view. Nor was it a matter of ideology only. The process was facilitated by the very condition of the text—polysemous, to be sure, but producing only *one* meaning in its quality as narrative structure orientated to the "saying of something about something." Multiple senses do not exist in one and the same reading. The rabbinical interpretation of Isaiah 53 cancels the interpretation made by the first Christians. It does not even admit it as a possible reading. And the same rabbinical reading replaced that practiced by the earlier one of the Septuagint. In other words, every reading involves a closure of meaning. What a paradox, this alternating play of polysemy in the text and monosemy in the reading! (See Diagram 3.)

Diagram 3
Distantiation 1, 2, and 3

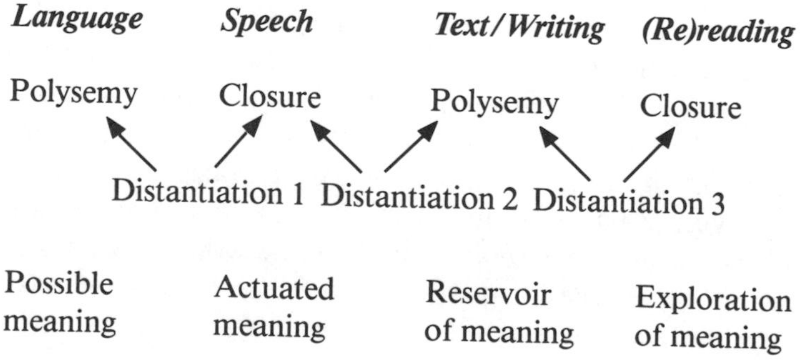

Language	*Speech*	*Text/Writing*	*(Re)reading*
Polysemy	Closure	Polysemy	Closure

Distantiation 1   Distantiation 2   Distantiation 3

Possible meaning	Actuated meaning	Reservoir of meaning	Exploration of meaning

The reading of the Bible made by liberation theology is also conflictual with respect to other "appropriations" of the meaning of the kerygma. There are several reasons for this, which I shall discuss in due time. But not the least of them is the "closuring" character of any reading. This is as basic as the phenomenon of textual dependency.

The conjunction between the meaning of a *text* and its "closuring" reading can lead to extreme situations with respect to other readings. Let us go back to the Targum of Isaiah 53. The interpretation it makes of the text of Isaiah (and what is relevant is that it be of Isaiah!) cannot be based on the Hebrew text of this prophet. The Aramaic version has had to modify the text *structurally,* transforming it into another account, distinct from the original, but reproduced in the synagogue reading as the authentic text of *Isaiah.* This rereading—more a midrash than a targum—entails a "closuring" and "erases" the account that would have allowed other readings.[23] The conflict of interpretations is vivid here, but it is not "spoken." One might wonder what the rabbis thought who also knew the Hebrew text, so different from the Aramaic version. But this question will lead us nowhere. The text that had become "tradition," and normative, was now none other than that of the targum. It was the canonical text of the moment. It is not the leadership, but the community, that receives a text as normative and *current.* It will be a different matter when the use of the targum is abandoned and the community returns to the Hebrew text, when Aramaic is no longer a living language for Palestinian Judaism. Now the polysemy of the Servant songs will give way to another reading, which, in its turn, will lay claim to absorbing the *whole* meaning, and once again exclude a christological interpretation.[24] We shall meet this same phenomenon in examining the hermeneutic act from the perspective of praxis, in chapter 2.

Let me conclude this subsection with two observations. First, the reader will have noticed that conflict of interpretations generates division, and one not always restricted to the theological level. Not all division is undesirable. Division can be creative. All-pervasive unity is sometimes amorphous and indolent. Secondly, "appropriation" of meaning, however much it may lay claim to totality, never actually achieves it. A text may have many interpretations, but all will have the same origin, and so of course there will be some form of convergence. The readings are in communication with one another through a sort of "underground." Division must be the division of something held in common, and thus it always preserves a factor of reunification. Myths, too, are mutually conflictual. Structured on the same theme, each nevertheless "crystalizes" within its own worldview, and lays claim to exhaust the meaning of the reality it interprets. But they communicate on the level of the symbols they weave together, as well as on that of a profound human experience.[25]

The Hermeneutic Function of Distantiation

I have mentioned two "distances"—one between language and speech, the other between speech and text or writing (see Diagram 2). The first is formal. The second is concrete, and in some manner temporal and spatial. The disappearance of the author of a text, the shift in addresses, changes in the life context engendering questions about the message—all these factors occasion a distantiation with respect to the first production of meaning, that of the act of discourse.

The greater the distance, the more numerous will be the perspectives of a rereading of the text. This will become more evident in chapter 2, when the "founding events" of a tradition are discussed. For the moment, I shall merely indicate that a *third* hermeneutic distantiation appears between the text, or writing, and its rereading (see Diagram 3). This distantiation appears between one reading and another: each begins with the *text* (which is obvious, because each is conditioned by the one preceding, the one it seeks to "erase"). Indeed, the later reading absorbs, or "subsumes," the earlier.

And so, in each reading, however conflictual, there is an element of convergence. At the same time, the chain of rereading of the Bible, or of any other text, ultimately results in an *accumulation of meaning*. The greater the distance, the more fertile the potential for plumbing the depths of the "reservoir of meaning" of a text. (We may say, therefore, that distantiation performs an interpretive function.)[26] From a "historicist" point of view, this is astounding, because distance appears to be inversely proportional to accuracy with respect to the original meaning. But from the hermeneutic point of view, distantiation is a fertile, creative phenomenon.

Summing up the results of the analyses in this chapter, Diagram 3 assimilates and completes Diagram 2.

2

Praxis and Interpretation

The question that now arises is: If a plurality of readings is viable, thanks to the linguistic conditioning of a text, what is it that concretely disengages and multiplies the readings?

FROM EVENT TO TEXT

The point of departure of a text is an experience of some kind—a practice, an important event, a worldview, a state of oppression, a liberation process, an experience of grace and salvation, or the like. Any of these may be called an "event." Even a natural phenomenon can qualify as an "event" in this sense, provided it has an impact on human life. In the infinite network of human practices and socio-historical experiences, some stand out as especially *significant*, for one reason or another, and they are thereupon gathered up in a *word*.

Two hermeneutic phenomena are at work at this moment. First, the word springing from the event, in order to narrate it or celebrate it, effectuates a selection, prioritizing one experience and leaving many others in shadow. This is a form of closure, and therefore of interpretation. *This* happening, not some other, calls for a word.

Secondly, this word *interprets* the event in the very act of narrating it. Never is it sheer chronicle, though it may make that pretense. There is no such thing as "pure" chronicle, without interpretation. Any reading of the "happenings" within an event is made from a standpoint, is made "in perspective." We know this, of course. But we need to delve into the implications of this phenomenon of selection-and-closure, this phenomenon of interpretation.

An event becomes significant for some *reason*, something in the context in which it takes place, something that gives it what we might call its "historical effect"—its influence on the practices of a particular human group.[27] It is not, be it noted, a matter of a simple cause-and-effect relationship, in which the cause may just as well disappear once the effect is produced, having no relationship of meaning with it. We are dealing with an event understood as the expression of the meaning of another event, which thereby takes shape as the "founding" event. The crossing of the Jordan in Joshua 3–5 is interpreted by Israelite tradition in the light of the crossing of the sea in the flight from Egypt—although no attempt is made to prove a causal connection between the two events. Hence the importance of distinguishing between causality and meaning.

It is clear, then, that an event can produce meaning, and that this meaning can be manifested in other events, aligned with the first. The first event, then, is seen as "originary" with respect to the others. It is now understood as the "founding" event. But it is seen to have been "founding" only at a distance—in light of its projections in new events. There is delay of a conferral of meaning. Taken up into a "word" as a significant fact, this event now manifests a "meaning surplus," which was not visible at the time of the physical event.

This is why any "historicist" reading of the biblical texts will be impoverishing. It will seek to read the facts as if they had occurred in the way in which they are recounted, and thus rob them of the hermeneutic distance that has restructured their meaning. The redactions of the biblical accounts as we have them today have the hermeneutic advantage of great distance from their events, and this distance has enriched them, charged them with meaning. And so once more we see the hermeneutic role of distantiation—which must not be restricted to a distantiation between texts: it also takes place with respect to the understanding of historical events. (The hermeneutic correspondence between these two levels of distantiation will be treated below).

An "originary event" broadens its meaning in readings made of it at a distance, as it incorporates new events (as the crossing of the Jordan is "retrojected" to the crossing of the sea in the exodus). But this is a "two-way street." The "enrichment reading" in turn invests with new meaning the events or practices from which it operates. The exodus "overspills" its signification onto the occupation of the promised land. The symbol of the crossing of the waters functions in both directions, and unites the events of originary liberation and present occupation of the land. We are dealing with another "hermeneutic circularity," then, the correlate of the one we observed in the interpretation of texts. This new circularity takes place in the first word that springs up and "says," bespeaks, the event, regardless of whether it presents itself as chronicle, epic poem, hymn, or in any other linguistic code. Even a festive celebration is a form of "reading" an event.

In the Bible, the "memory" of the event of deliverance from slavery in Egypt is re-presented in every possible literary genre, and in every age. But it is never a repetition of the meaning of the originary exodus. It is always a scanning of its "reservoir of meaning." The events influencing the formation of a people are not exhausted in their first narration. They "enlarge" in meaning, by way of their projections into the life of that people. But in order to express this "meaning surplus," the "word" of the event "redimensions" and reworks the event: the call of Moses, the plagues over the land of Egypt, the hasty Passover, the crossing of the sea—these are *not* episodes of the liberation event, but expressions of its *meaning*, as *God's* design and activity, or as memorial celebration (Passover). If the exodus had occurred as it is related to have occurred, we would have a "documentary," not an interpretation—just some happening or other, without *theological* significance, "fantastic" divine presence. No, the Hebrew people lived that liberation experience (which did not have to be *externally* strange or wondrous) as a "design" in continuous course of realization. It felt the need to "refer" to this event, to "go back" to it, in order to recover its hope when it fell into the clutches of an oppressor, or in order to deepen its faith-in-gratitude when it celebrated new liberative situations.

Foundational Events

It is noteworthy that, among most peoples, national patriotic festivals tend to be celebrations of *liberation* events. Latin America furnishes us with good examples. These events have been erected into founding, or archetypal, events, in an interpretive process, in the course of the development of the history of these peoples. The "memory" of an occurrence recharges it with meaning. It is the meaning itself of the events which are generated, whether because of a causal linkage or simply by way of interpretation. The exodus did not generate the return from the Babylonian captivity. Yet Hebrew tradition interprets the latter as a new exodus (see Isa. 11:15–16; 19:16–25; 43:16–21; 51:9–11).[28] The original exodus reveals a deeper dimension of signification when the Israelites recall it as a liberative undertaking in new situations of oppression or captivity. The inexhaustibility of its inspiration and meaning is apparent in the *readings* that the Hebrew people, and later the Christian community, and today the theology of liberation, make of it. In like manner, peoples look to their own foundational events (such as deeds of liberation) as inspiration and meaning for their socio-historical praxis, at least when there is a national consciousness and a collective undertaking for release from alien domination.

Here a "conflict of interpretations," which was discussed in connection with the reading of texts (in chapter 1), can reappear. The same conflict occurs in the reading of events, whether because these always contain a meaning surplus that is not exhausted in their first realization—they are polysemous, and there is no reason why their interpretations should coincide—or because they are interpreted from different standpoints and in different circumstances. And as we know, each interpretation is "totalizing"—exclusive, seeking to appropriate *all* meaning.

The struggles of a people for its independence are read both to motivate a liberation process and to legitimate its repression. One reading excludes the other, but both go back to a single "originary," "significative" event. The readings are made in function of different practices—the "loci" from which the event is read—hence their conflictuality. No interpretation is innocent, flawlessly objective. An interpreted event is never objective. This does not imply that the *reading* is subjective. There must be *something* in the event that permits the derivation of such-and-such an interpretation. What is decisive is the *praxis* that generates the reading. The concepts of objectivity and subjectivity are of singularly little utility in the analysis of what occurs in the hermeneutic act.

The other side of the coin of the conflict of interpretations is the *conflict of practices* inspired by the interpreted event. On account of the latter conflict, the sequence of event-to-word, which we have been analyzing, does not end here, in the word. There are more links in the chain. But before pursuing this analysis further, some of the points already made must be reemphasized.

From Closure to Polysemy

We must be especially careful to grasp the fact that, in the hermeneutic phenomenon of the "event become word," we find ourselves faced once more with an alternation of polysemous meaning and monosemous meaning—with a cycle from reservoir of meaning to meaning closure and back again, the same phenomenon observable with respect to language in its semiotic and hermeneutic aspects. We shall encounter this alternation throughout the process that I am about to explain. What must be kept in mind is that, in each link of the chain, the order is *from closure to polysemy*. In other words, the event with which a chain begins is polysemous, but the "word" interpreting it is a closure of its meaning. (Otherwise it would not be an intelligible reading, and so would not be a message.) But in the second moment, this "word" opens up once more to another reading: being in some fashion a "text," it recovers its polysemous value (see Diagram 4).

Diagram 4
The Many Readings of an Event:
From Polysemy to Closure to Polysemy

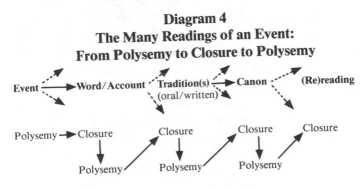

The event is open to many readings, each of which closes the meaning, only to have it opened once more, and so on; the process can be repeated many, many times.

Tradition

The second observation that must be made—without prejudice to a more explicit treatment in chapter 3—has to do with the theological consequences of the hermeneutic fact that the "event becomes word." In the case of the Bible, this means that this book, before it was the *word* of God, was an *event* of God. Israel's salvific experience is interpreted in an account that sets in relief a presence of God that was surely not such as is set forth in literary fashion.

Within a particular group of persons, this account is transformed into a living *tradition*. The distance with respect to its first inscription of meaning now opens it to a rereading. This is why the "closuring word" of the message of an event becomes polysemous in a second moment. The hermeneutic process continues. Tradition, then, in all its many forms, from determinate practices to oral or written texts, is the organized rereading of earlier readings of founding events. By "organized" I mean that the rereading is a social structuration of practices, myths, or accounts concerning the origins, worldviews, laws, rites, and so on, that weld a human group together. This can be exemplified in the case of Israel, other religions, or philosophical, political, or any other traditions. Social reality and the hermeneutic phenomenon underlying it are interrelated, in all cases. The dimensions or numerousness of the traditions in question are of no concern here. The Yahwist tradition of the Pentateuch must have been in conflict with the Elohist in their first encounter. But in the redaction in which we have them, they converge in a new tradition, one that embraces them both without conflict. This phenomenon has a thousand ramifications.

I speak of tradition in general, then, in order to illustrate what occurs on the level of interpretation, beginning with a significative event. As any tradition, or any moment in a larger tradition, comes in conflict with another current tradition that goes back to the same interpreted occurrence, we find ourselves faced once more with what I call the struggle for the appropriation of meaning, with all the pretensions—on the part of this appropriation—to totality and exclusivity.

At a certain stage, tradition, representing the closure of an earlier reading of originary events, tends to become polysemous—open to interpretation. No living tradition is static. Immobility would be its death. But the very concept of "tradition" implies a limiting, controlling context, a staking out of boundaries. Its rereading will frequently mean division. When a tradition arrives at the moment of greatest tension in its growth of meaning, one of two possible solutions generally results. Either it divides or it "closures" in a *canon*—which will also exclude aspects of tradition, thus being tantamount to originating a certain division.

Canon

The appearance of a "canon" of writings is a phenomenon of all tradition—religious, philosophical, historical, political, or what have you. There is a need to establish the authentic texts of Plato, Thomas Aquinas, and Marx, as well as of the sacred books of religion (the Vedas, the Qur'ān, the Bible, or such-and-such a cycle of myths). It might be thought that in religions having no scriptures there would be no canon; but myths are not without their limits, are not incoherent among themselves within a given religious worldview. On the contrary, they are perfectly coherent, and mutually explanatory—being, as a whole, semantically irreducible to those of another worldview. This is a form of canon. Only, it is a canon of myths, not of writings. In either case, what we have are *texts*.

Forming a canon is a phenomenon of "closure": it excludes other readings of an earlier tradition even as it orients the interpretation of new practices. Every closure of a canon is part of a long hermeneutic process. At a determinate moment in the course of this process, a "cut-off," a delimitation occurs, with respect to the (oral or written) texts representing *the* interpretation of the events that have given rise to this tradition. If there are a good many texts, they are gathered up as a totality that, from a linguistic standpoint, constitutes a single new text. Thus from "*inter*textuality" (the interrelationships among texts, one myth understood in light of another within the same community, and so on) we move to "*intra*textuality" (now these relationships obtain *within* one larger text). In this way, the Bible finally comes to be *a* book, so that,

from Genesis to Revelation, we now have *one* total kerygmatic meaning, its multiple variations or manifestations not-
withstanding. This explains how there can be so many disparate traditions in the Bible, so many different theological
currents, and yet they do not hamper its acceptance. The same
observation can be made with respect to the internal content
of each book, which itself gathers up earlier traditions into a
new whole. In all cases, there is a transformation of an
intertextuality into a new, intratextual relationship.

One more reflection is called for regarding canonicity. The
constitution of a canon is accompanied by some form of
division. The Samaritan canon of scripture (reduced to the
Pentateuch) was opposed to the Judean canon in force in the
south, where the selection of the sacred texts was made, let us
make no mistake, in conformity with political, and not only
religious, criteria. In A.D. 90, the rabbis at the Council of
Jamnia, near present-day Tel Aviv, established a "definitive"
canon of sacred books, because they felt the need to curb the
growth of religious texts and to oppose the formation of a
Christian literature, which was a rereading of the Old Testament. The sacred books, it was decided, would be the ones
currently considered as such if written in Palestine, in Hebrew
or Aramaic, no later than the time of Ezra, and not supporting
Christians in their christological reading of the Old Testament.
This decision sealed the division between the rabbinical and
the Christian canons. It also divided the Jewish community in
at least two ways: the Alexandrine canon—the Septuagint—
used by Jews of Greek culture was rejected; and rejections
must have been provoked on the part of Palestinian Jewish
groups as well, entailing their own exclusion from the larger
religious community.

The formation of the New Testament canon, as well, knew
its vicissitudes, oppositions, and divisions. During the Protes-
tant Reformation, still another division in the canon was
created, this time with respect to the books of the Old Testament, with the Protestants taking up the Hebrew canon of the

Jewish tradition and the Catholics and Orthodox the Alexandrine canon of the Seputagint, which the church had used since the days of its initial expansion into the world of Greek language and culture. Again, the same hermeneutic phenomenon is at play. Only content and names have changed.

Diagram 5
Linguistic and Praxic Vectors of a Text

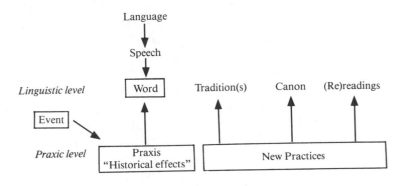

The "word" that interprets an event (word-account or text) has a linguistic vector "coming" as language and "going" as tradition, canon, or new reading. It also has a praxic vector, which, once it has converged with the linguistic, develops and engages in mutual re-creation with it. The "word" marks the transition from linguistics to hermeneutics.

At this point we come again to the level of language—where we started. The meaning-*event* is subsumed into a meaning-*text*, which has the status of *scripture*. "Word" moves us to the plane of language (see Diagram 5). But the arrival on the scene of the canon reinforces the inscription of the message in a written, fixed text. The salvific events experienced by the people of Israel are present once more, this time as read, heard, and interpreted in the form in which they have been mediated and transmitted by earlier readings, which converge in *one* current text (in intratextuality, then) that becomes normative.

Inspiration

My analysis thus far allows me to make some observations on the subject of inspiration. The relevance conferred on the biblical text because it is *God's revelation* has tended to detract attention from the human process of its production. The theology of biblical inspiration is based on the fact of revelation, as contained in the sacred books we call the Bible. This theology has focused on the datum that God inspires the *authors* writing books that later came to form the biblical canon. This inspiration is a guarantee of inerrancy. Eventually the limits of this inerrancy came to be disputed, without a great deal of attention to the matter of linguistic codes.

In the light of what we have seen of semiotics and hermeneutics, this emphasis on the *authors* of the texts seems off the mark. It ignores the fact that the author "dies" in the production of a text. We read a *text*, not an author. To conceive of biblical inspiration as attaching to the sacred writers is a form of historicism, and this sacred halo leaves the text more unprotected than might be supposed. In the first place, what could possibly be the point of a *re*reading of these texts, which presupposes a reservoir of meaning that the author did not foresee?

A second defect in the traditional doctrine of inspiration can be likened to a "short circuit." Inspiration is conceptualized as flowing from God-speaking, to the sacred writer, to the text. God inspires the sacred writer to write the text. But as we have seen, the canonical text has its point of departure in "God-acting," God's activity in history. God-speaking—the "word of God"—is the *reading*, through the lens of faith, of the God of salvation history. If inspiration has to do with the veracity of the biblical texts, then it should not be considered to attach to the authors but to the texts themselves. Inspiration is better understood as a *textual* phenomenon. If the text is what is inspired, any rereading of the Bible recovers a meaning that is somehow inspired, even if that meaning is part of the "reservoir of meaning" that was not in the intention of the author.

Canonicity and Re-creation

The canon has not closed everything. That would be wishful thinking. If the canon intends to close the meaning of an event-account, then at that very instant it exerts pressure on the polysemy of the event, and indeed of the account. There is a meaning surplus that overflows and must be taken up in new practices and new words. New events will be experienced in the light of the normative scriptures, it is true. But at the same time they outstrip these scriptures. What happens at this point, if the canon is a closure that does not admit a reopening, or the inclusion of new traditions? Let us make no mistake. The canon will be polysemous. After all, it is a *text*. To think that its interpretation stops with the formation of the canon is preposterous.

There are several possibilities. The canonical text cannot be modified or expanded. But a commentary may appear, for example. Thus the Upanishads are an interpretation of the "revelation" (*sruti*, in Sanskrit) contained in the Vedas, as will be the later Vedanta. The Talmud is the authoritative commentary on the Torah. The writings of the fathers of the church are an authoritative interpretation of the Christian canon, and so on. There is a "canon" of the texts of Marx, too; but then come the interpretations, plural.

Of course, besides commentary, there are other kinds of literature that survive the constitution of an unmodifiable sacred text. A targum is an attenuated rereading. A midrash is a new text interpreting an old text in view of new situations. The little data we have on the infancy of Moses (Exod. 2) are expanded into a midrash. The same thing happens with the infancy accounts of Jesus (Matt. 1–2; Luke 1–2). And there are other early apocryphal, or extracanonical, writings that "fill in" the life of Jesus. They attempt to bring the sacred text to situations not clearly contemplated in it.

At times the re-creative force of an event-account (the New Testament as a rereading of the Old) is so great that, due to the conflict of interpretations involved, it enters into the canon-forming process. But this can be initiated only by the group that does the authoritative rereading of the Old Testament—the Christian church. The result is that the Christian canon comes into conflict with the Jewish canon. Both readings lay claim to an appropriation of the meaning of salvific happenings, and so, of course, division ensues. As we see, the history of the canon of scripture is part of a hermeneutic process, and the latter is part of the history of traditions.

The canon is not the beginning of a tradition, then, nor is it its end. It is a moment in a continuous journey. To speak of the "inspiration of the canon" is a new hermeneutical act. It is an interpretation of the closure of meaning that is the historical option of a community, an option seen as dictated by God. From this point on, it is impossible to add or subtract a single book to or from the normative canon. As we have remarked, however, the interpretive process cannot be closed off. A long process of literary production is generated, from a simple translation (like that of the Septuagint and others), to targum, *pesher,* or midrash. A targum is a translation of the Hebrew text into Aramaic, but with certain hermeneutic liberties that introduce indispensable updating elements of the message into the translation. *Pesher* is a commentary on a biblical text, verse by verse, or selected passages. A verse is quoted and then the commentary begins: "The explanation is . . ." or "Its explanation is . . . ." *Pesher* is a characteristic literary genre of the Dead Sea scrolls.[29] It is a form of rereading of the canonical text. Midrash, as already stated above, is the free expansion of a biblical text in the form of a new story. Midrash is a part of the rabbinical literature that goes back to the time of Jesus, if not earlier. There are a great number of midrashim. But besides being a literary genre, midrash is a hermeneutic method used to explain the deeper meaning of a biblical text. In this case, it is called *darash*.[30]

These are examples of an overflow of a canon once its traditional or official immutability has been established. But there is also the exegetical commentary, or homily, on the biblical texts, or the theological and philosophical systematizations inscribed in one tradition to the exclusion of others. Thus the canon, which in the moment of its constitution was an expression of "closure of meaning," ironbound and authoritarian, becomes polysemous, in virtue of being a text, in virtue of the distance between it and the successive generations who read it, and in virtue of the life of the community that harbors it. This short survey has shown several ways in which a rereading can bring out meanings of a text that is no longer to be rewritten.

The rereading of the Bible is not effectuated only as a literary work, by specialists. This is never the case. Neither was the midrash or the *pesher* the product of the specialization of rabbis or doctors of the law. They were generated in a community, in many communities, or within the theological currents of religious groups.

The exegete's aspiration—sometimes rendered explicit—of isolating the objective, *historical* sense of a biblical text is illusory. Furthermore, neither is it such a simple matter to get at what is "behind" the text. This is the exegete's claim, but it is a false claim when what are used are simply historico-critical methods uncomplemented by literary criticism in a broad sense, or by semiotics and hermeneutics. What the exegete is really exploring are the possibilities residing *in the text* for its interpretation in an ever novel way. We are presented with an analysis of the thought *of Paul* in one of his letters; but Paul is known only through his texts. No exegete ever knew him otherwise. It is a different matter when historical criticism can contribute extratextual elements to our knowledge of the author of a text or of an author's cultural context. This is altogether positive, as I emphasized in the Introduction. But the reservoir of meaning residing in a text does not depend on this knowledge. It depends on the *text*, and on the *life* that gives orientation to the question addressed to that text. This is what I have been maintaining, and what I shall continue to maintain, as the objective of this book.

It must also be acknowledged that exegetes are immersed in a tradition, in a historical context—that they are the subject of determinate social practices. All this conditions their reading as a *rereading*. The church does the same thing in interpreting the word of God. Its reading is "closuring," for it is made from a certain locus—in other words, from a given practice, simultaneously religious and political. And the people? Its reading of the Bible is mediated by that of "knowers"—theologians, specialists—or "rulers"—church authority. But when the people approaches the Bible (often forbidden) without those mediations, its reading is one of unsuspected fecundity. And when this occurs in a liberation process, or some other situation in which the people or a community is the subject both of history and of its own reading of the biblical kerygma—what happens then? This question brings us to a new point in the endeavor to plumb the phenomenon of the rereading of the Bible.

The findings of this section are summed up in Diagram 4 (see p. 41).

THE "FORWARD" OF A TEXT

All reading is production of meaning, and is done from a locus or context. As a result, what is genuinely relevant is not the "behind" of a text, but its "ahead," its "forward"—what it suggests as a pertinent message for the life of the one who receives or seeks it out. Polysemous text that it is, its reading is always exploratory. The text unfolds "to the fore," displaying a "world" of possibilities, which readers bring into harmony with their own "world." Whether we call this phenomenon a "fusion of horizons" (H.G. Gadamer) or give it some other name, what is important is the fact that the "forward" of a text makes it impossible for its past meaning to be "eternalized"—as if it were the *only* meaning just because it has been closured.

The Bible is an open text. Precisely as a *text*, it is open. This must be kept in mind if we wish it to be a message for today. The ones most in need of the liberative message of the Bible, the oppressed of every sort and kind, are those who have had least access to it. Thus what we call a "rereading of the Bible"—one aspect of the complex phenomenon of hermeneutics—is of special concern to them. Accordingly, a conscientization with respect to the implications of hermeneutic theory is vital for the theology of liberation—the reflection on faith that is done from within a context of the hopes and struggles of the oppressed.

Such a reading of the Bible from the "grass roots," from the "base," will entail certain difficulties and certain advantages. Let me point out two disadvantages. The Bible, first of all, is a very long book. It contains "a bit of everything," and one can find pretty much whatever one would like. Do narrative semiotics and hermeneutics have a contribution to make here? Indeed they do, as we shall see.

Secondly, the Bible is a book put together and structured, by and large, by a comfortable middle class generally alienated from the people. This is more visible in the Old Testament, where the ideology of the south—of Judah, and of Jerusalem in particular, where the governing class resided—is set in high relief. This general situation is prolonged, down through the centuries, in the process of catechetical and theological transmission. Classic theology had the resources to reproduce itself *ad infinitum*, and could not break out from its own circularity.

What would be the advantage of the Bible, as it has been handed down, when it comes to a creative, liberative reading? There is one that is priceless. Its origin, in the origin of the Israelites as a people, was *in a liberation process*. The

Israelite conception of Yahweh, the God of the Hebrew people, is indissolubly joined to the experience of deliverance from slavery in Egypt. In that context, the *savior* God is identified with the *liberator* God. After narrating the deed of the flight from Egypt, the sacred text comments: "When Israel . . . beheld the great power that the Lord had shown against the Egyptians, they feared the Lord and *believed* in him and in his servant Moses" (Exod. 14:30–31). That was a "believing" that arose out of the experience of liberation.

From this moment forward, it is this liberation experience that will be the "referent" in the historico-salvific project of Israel. Accordingly, in the account of Moses' call to be the leader of the liberation of the Hebrews (Exod. 3:1–20)—an account which is also a "word" *of the event* of the exodus as reread down through uncounted generations—Moses is assured that the God who speaks will "be with" him in the liberation struggle (Exod. 3:12). The "I am" of the gloss in Exodus 3:13–14 is not the "am" of existence, but the "am" of presence—not like the Spanish *ser*, but like *estar*—and identifies Yahweh as a God who "is with" Moses and Israel. It is a commentary on verse 12, linking the familiar name "Yahweh" with the divine salvific presence in this great event.[31] The concept of the God of the Bible is a rereading of the experience of the exodus.

Jewish religious institutions—the festivals, the prophetical critique of breaches of the covenant, the heralding of a new order of justice, the messianic hope, Jesus' proclamation—all these, too, recall and retrieve the "memory" of the exodus as liberative content. Even what had been taken over from the worldview of a mythical universe will now have a new sense: the temple, many of the rituals, language about Yahweh, and the like, so often a transfer of the symbolic language of the religions of Israel's neighbors (especially in hymnology, and in the prophetical dispute over the identity of Yahweh).

This complexus, in order to reinforce a theology of the God of liberation, assimilates theologoumena from the worldviews held by Israel's neighbors concerning God (and God's vicar, the king) as distributor and guarantor of justice and the well-being of the nation.[32] And the whole constitutes a "semantic axis" on the level of text, which becomes, at the proper moment, a "kerygmatic axis" on the level of message. The latter, central to the Old Testament, is then projected into the New, in the salvific message of Jesus addressed *preferentially* to the poor of every sort and manner—in his options for the poor, in his death as a prophet rejected for his words and deeds.

Here the programatic scenario of Luke 4:16–30 should be referred to, where Jesus rereads, as "fulfilled" in himself, the great text of Isaiah 61:1-2 on the proclamation of the good news to the poor, the delivery of captives, sight to the blind, and freedom to the oppressed (Luke 4:18). The account closes with another mention of the "good news" (v. 43)— ever the message to the poor and oppressed, and not with some generic, diffuse, or random content. And the final words: ". . . Because this is why I was sent" (ibid.). Is this option for the oppressed not preferential, perhaps indeed exclusive?[33]

The Paschal mystery, on which the whole of the Christian kerygma hinges, can be interpreted along different lines by the New Testament accounts precisely in virtue of its reservoir of meaning as event and as text of the tradition that culminates in the narration of the Gospels: in one form or another, the various approaches are all expressions of the power of the hope of liberation, so firmly settled in the consciousness of the people of the Bible.[34] Even with its contextual transfer, the liberation message permeates the pages of the New Testament. And the theology of the exodus—sometimes, to be sure, at a distance—echoes once again.

INTRATEXTUALITY

New Meaning in New Totalizations

The development of my theme obliges me to introduce a precision, originating in semiotics but of profit for hermeneutics. "Narrative semiotics" teaches us that the message of a text is not in a fragment of the account, but in its totality, as structure codifying a meaning. In the account of the sacrifice of Isaac, for example, in Genesis 22, there is no "main sentence" to manifest the signification of the episode. The whole narrative sequence enters into the production of meaning by a subsequent reading. But when one account is woven, "textured," with another, a *new* account is produced that is not the sum of its parts, and the meaning will be in this new codified totality, now constituting one text, and not in the sum of the literary units or their original significations. The production of meaning is modified successively as texts join one another, with intertextuality growing into a greater intratextuality.

With the help of critical methods, additions to or interpolations in the text can be recognized. In Psalm 78, verse 9 fails to harmonize with the context. A reader who would read the psalm without this verse would find a hymn of national confession of sins, with the emphasis on the breach of the covenant and infidelity to the law. The verbs in the third person plural of verses 10–11, and so on, would refer to the "fathers," the generation of the exodus and the sojourn in the wasteland (see vv. 4b–7). Then, in a second reading, the one that has come down to us, verse 9 is inserted: "The sons of Ephraim, ordered ranks of bowmen, retreated in the day of battle." This has nothing to do with what the hymn has been saying. But it produces an effect on the order of structural meaning: the verbs that follow, from verse 10 on, now refer to the Ephraimites, the Israelites of the north. Thus the entire psalm is modified in its structure and in its message. This shift receives its seal in the complementary verses 67–72, extolling the election of Judah and Jerusalem, or the ideology of the south, and rejecting the Israel of the north.

Which text ought we to read today? Surely, the current form, however little it may be to our taste. The critical reconstruction of the account helps us set its new redaction in relief. But the addition is *no longer* an addition in the text as it has been handed down. It is a new text, and it produces meaning *as it is.* And it will always have its hermeneutic "forward"—what it says to us from a new horizon, from a "new intratextuality."

The transition from intertextuality to intratextuality is excellently illustrated in the Book of Amos. This prophetical account is universally recognized to be divided into two sections, of contradictory tenor. Amos 1:1–9:10 consists entirely of various oracles addressed to Israel by way of criticism and denunciation of the social sins of the powerful perpetrated against the lowly. But 9:11–15 proclaims the restoration of the Davidic dynasty and great future prosperity. There is everything to indicate that these final verses constitute a later addition. Indeed, their images, content, and opposition to the tenor of the rest of the book are proof enough. But what are we to conclude? To shrug it all off as the juxtaposition of oracles from different times by an inattentive redactor would be the "easy way out." Instead, what we ought to recognize here is a linguistic fact and hermeneutic phenomenon of profound theological value. After all, the Book of Amos as we have it today is *a single text*, and must be read as such if the reader is to grasp its message. It matters little that it is no longer the text of the historical Amos. But it is a *text of Amos.*

The final oracles of salvation *modify* the narrative positioning, and thereby the signification, of the oracles of punishment. What these latter may have meant *earlier*—either in their proclamation by the prophet or as a literary composition (definitive judgment and the destruction of the people of Israel)—*now* mean that that punishment is not to be definitive and irrevocable, but is in conformity with a more fundamental intention, that of keeping God's promise alive: God cannot endure the sin and falsehood or injustice (Amos 1–9) that nullify the historical undertaking that comes to light in the liberation of the exodus (see Amos 2:6–16). Israel will not be converted by the prophetical denunciation; it will be converted in the suffering of its downfall.[35] It is here that it will recover its fidelity to the God of liberation, who, once more, will deliver Israel from a new oppression, that of the Babylonian exile.

To repeat: Amos 1:1–9:15 is a *single* text, to be read as a narrational and structural totality modifying the message of its integrated parts. In other words, it would not have been the same if 9:11–15 had been a separate text or a part of the great narrative sequence in the account of Amos 1:1–9:15. As a hermeneutic phenomenon, the text of Amos gives us to understand that the *event* of the captivity, or the situation of the dominated Judeans of postexilic times, led them to reinterpret the prophet's old message (become reality now), in the light of a new hope of liberation.

Meanwhile, readers will have realized that the final redaction is no longer addressed to the kingdom of the north, to Israel. Now it is addressed to Judah. The rereading effectuated this shift. To reread is not to drain the meaning. It is to explore the superabundance latent in its textual polysemy. With singular clarity, Amos 9:11–15 takes the demand for justice of 1:1–9:10 as a kerygmatic nucleus, and projects it into the proclamation of a new stage of salvation history.

The Bible: A Single Text

What this example has shown us, on a small scale, can be extended to the whole Bible. In a way, *the Bible is a single text*, especially from the moment it constituted a fixed canon of literary compositions. This closure establishes new relationships among its different parts, and among its distinct literary collections—legal, historical, prophetical, sapiential, evangelical, epistolary, apocalyptic, and so on. Like any structured work, it has a beginning and an end—and an ordered progression between them. It runs from Genesis to Revelation along a particular route.

The juxtaposition of the Jewish canon and the primitive Christian body of texts has its own "meaning effect." To continue to speak of an "Old" and a "New" Testament has its practical utility for distinguishing textual blocks, traditions, and eras, but it undermines the hermeneutic effort of the primitive church to constitute a *single* text. Thus it is better to employ such terms as "Bible" and "Scriptures." Nor is it possible to be an "Old Testament expert" or a "New Testament expert." This is semiotic dismemberment. One may devote oneself *more* to one part of the Bible than to another. But studying or teaching the "Old Testament" without entering into the so-called New Testament, or to study or teach the latter without seeking its roots in the so-called Old Testament, is to effectuate an epistemological rupture that cancels the meaning of the New Testament as a rereading of the traditions of Israel. Ironically, it would be a new rereading of the Bible as two distinct works—a strange thing indeed.

If the Bible, then, is a *single* text, it is not the cumulative sum of a plurality of literary units. It is the unification of a linguistically coded central kerygma. Henceforth it is possible to recognize, in this one, *extended* account, the "semantic axes" orientating the production of meaning that is our reading of the Bible. This is an all but new undertaking, and of inestimable importance, especially in view of the difficulty to which I called attention at the beginning of the last section above—the extent and diversity of theological traditions and concepts in the Bible. At the end of the same section I suggested what one of these "axes of meaning" in the Bible as a totality would be: the kerygma of the liberation of the oppressed. Other "axes" structuring the Bible as a single, lengthy account would be those of justice, love and fidelity, hope, the covenant, prophecy, God's presence as grace, judgment, freedom, and so on. The hermeneutic enterprise does not consist in listing relevant *themes*. It consists in the *structuration* of these themes in the total work that is the Bible.

Taking the Bible as *one* text will enrich our fragmentary readings of individual pericopes or books. At the same time, a purely *lexicological* approach will have to be rejected, because it transfers the message from the account as a totality to the words in their semantic value—sometimes a regression to the stage of language or the dictionary! Words have meaning only in a text that closures that meaning. Where a larger account contains many smaller accounts, the meaning of one and the same word will vary. The word "justice," for instance, does not have a constant meaning throughout the Bible. It would be an error of perspective, sometimes actually committed, to force the meaning of words, and forget that what is important is not the word, but the account. When I speak of "semantic axes," I am not asserting that "justice," "liberation," and so on, have a single meaning all the way through the Bible. I mean that, in the Bible as a narrative totality, there is a new production of meaning, where many meanings of certain words or ideas, in their de facto literary contexts, are structured in such a way that they produce a new meaning effect.

The quest for "semantic axes" in the Bible is a new reading—a hermeneutic reading, of course, but with a debt to semiotics. There are biblical narrations, for example, or separate texts, representing the king as the vicar of God, designated by God to rule over Israel; and there are other texts pointing to the king as Yahweh's rival, or criticizing him as unfaithful to his office. There are texts that reject authority, and others that extol obedience to authority. In the totality of the Bible, however, is not power—the king's, a judge's, and so on—an instrument to save the weak, to help those who do not have power and therefore are exploited, who do not have power and therefore cannot free themselves? On the whole, is the Bible not also saying that power, in human hands, is fragile, and easily corrupted—that it degenerates into oppressive power?

We would do well to recall that the synagogue understood the canon of scriptures as a totality. Texts alluding to the "law" refer not to the Pentateuch alone, but to all the scriptures, considering them as one great, divine collection of statutes for Israel. Similarly, the term "prophets" at times refers to the totality of those books of the canon that are understood in terms of an eschatological message. This was the outlook of the primitive church, as well, which *reread* the whole Old Testament as a *single text* (on the semiotic level) with a single hermeneutic key (the Easter mystery). This rereading did not involve despoiling the Old Testament of less suitable books, or of passages that validate the law and sometimes even contradict Christian praxis (like the custom of the anathema, *herem*; or the ideal of Israel's dominion over other nations, as in Deut. 15:6, Isa. 60:12, and so on). We might have expected that the Book of Leviticus would be eliminated, along with so many other texts regulating the priestly order, which the Christians discontinued. But this did not occur. The so-called Old Testament, as a unit, is the word of God, overflowing the contextualization of each passage as such and orientated to a kerygmatic *telos*, Christ (Gal. 3:24; Rom. 10:4).

Had it abbreviated the Jewish canon, the church would have been producing an *other* text, whose reading could no longer be an appropriation of meaning of the traditions of Israel. This was a decisive point, because the infant church had no consciousness of a distinctive "founding"; it understood itself as the reinterpretation *of Israel.* Indeed, for the first Christians their rereading was *the* interpretation of Israel's traditions (an awaited hermeneutic closure), as we see in the appropriation of the whole symbolism of Israel in the Christian writings (canonical and patristic), in the missionary effort to show that Jesus was the Messiah awaited by Israel, in the first preaching to the Jews, and so on. The church, then, was the new *Israel*, and had to reread Israel's scriptures as a totality so as to be able to find great "centers of gravity" in them.

Rabbinical exegesis was more attached to short texts and individual words (consider the Talmud), but Christian exegesis sought to harmonize the whole meaning of the scriptures. It had taken a position within the intratextuality of these scriptures, thereupon setting it in contiguity with new texts— gospels, letters, and others—which were its rereading, and thus forming a new intertextuality (because now these earlier scriptures, with their intratextuality, are interrelated with new ones). At our distance, our own rereading should take up the whole Bible once more in its character as a new intratextuality, so that we may discover its new semantic axes, and be able to read it from within our own lives.

TO WHOM DOES THE BIBLE "PERTAIN" AND "BELONG"?

I have alluded above to the fact that the Bible comports an advantage for its reading from the standpoint of the oppressed, or of liberation—namely, that its origin was marked by profound experiences of suffering and oppression, liberation and grace, in which Israelite faith could recognize the savior God in a liberative dimension. This faith-in-gratitude, faith and acknowledgment of God as savior, was eventually subsumed in "professions of faith" (Deut. 6:20–24; 26:5–9, and so forth), in the great accounts, in the prophets, in worship. The tradition of Israel prolonged this thematic over so many centuries because the people experienced so many processes of oppression-and-liberation down through those centuries. Even in its latest historical stage, coinciding with the formation of the sacred texts as such (the postexilic era), the nation was under the political domination of foreign empires—the Persian, the Seleucid, the Roman—and the economic oppression of burdensome external and internal tributes to be paid.

This sociological factor helps us contextualize the fixation of the ancient traditions of oppression-and-liberation in codes of history and promise. The situation described in Nehemiah 9 is fraught with meaning. With the return from exile of a caravan of former captives, the new community completes its process of organization. The text centers this event on the law. A politically dominated nation has no other way of striking an internal cohesion but the religious way: worship, a temple, sacred institutions, all expressed in a code of laws. And so Nehemiah celebrates a renewal of the covenant (Neh. 8–10). Its "historical prologue" consists of a commentary on God's actions from creation to the history of Israel, with its recent situation of suffering and great sorrow and discouragement, also seen as the product of divine intervention.[36] In fact, the hymn of Nehemiah 9 takes the literary form of a "national confession of sins," as it is called, in which the hope of liberation is reaffirmed. Hence the eloquent finale:

> But, see, we *today* are *slaves*; and as for the *land which you gave* our fathers that they might eat its fruits and good things—see, we have become *slaves upon it!* Its rich produce *goes to the kings* whom you set over us [whatever rulers happened to be exercising domination over the Jews, one hegemony after another] because of our sins, who rule over our bodies and our cattle as they please. We are in great distress! [Neh. 9:36–37; emphasis added].

Observe that this is the same situation as is reflected in the final structure of the Pentateuch. The Pentateuch is the book of promise, of hope, which even tells of the deed of liberation from Egypt as a *departure for* the promised land—that is, for the realization of those promises (the land, a people, a heritage). And yet the Pentateuch closes *without* narrating this fulfillment. Everything ends on the banks of the Jordan, on the plains of Moab, facing Jericho. Certain exegetes have attempted to resolve this paradox with the hypothesis of a Hexateuch—six books, then, including Joshua—for which there is not a shred of further evidence.

Actually, the paradox is easy to explain. The Pentateuch was completed at a critical moment in the history of Israel, after the tremendous setback represented by the exile, with the nation only then entering into a stage of reorganization, deprived of any political or economic independence, with only a remnant of the people, and a land invaded and occupied. In this situation, the promise to the fathers is *still open*. The people has not yet arrived in the land of liberty. It is still on a journey, in the hope of seeing its end. If the Pentateuch had closed with the conquest of the land, it would have been a document of the past. In its actual state, it is the relaunching of hope in the fulfillment of a promise. The structure, then, is part of the message.[37] In other words, the Pentateuch was closured from the viewpoint of the oppressed. Is this not a tremendously important observation for a modern rereading of the Pentateuch, when human beings find themselves in so many situations of such great sorrow and discouragement, of "unfulfillment," of unrealized hopes, frustration, and all manner of oppression? This is the other side of the coin of the "semantic axis" of the Bible as a single extended text.

And so I must once more assert my conviction that the principal origin of the Bible is in experiences of suffering-and-oppression and grace-and-liberation, and that it is written with a profound hope of salvation. This does not mean that it is not addressed to all. No one is excluded. All social classes are interdependent. There are texts in the Bible addressed explicitly to the wealthy, to oppressors—and the poor and oppressed hear these texts *as so addressed*, because their status in life is conditioned by that of the privileged. The Bible sets in high relief God's preference for the oppressed, the marginalized, the sick, sinners, and so on. Its message is received by them as hope. At the same time, it is received by those who are responsible for this reality, but in their case it is received as judgment—or as an invitation to conversion.

Inasmuch as the generality of human experience is that of suffering, wretchedness, sin, and oppression, it is not difficult to recognize that the most adequate "ownership" of the Bible, the most adequate "pertinency" for rereading the kerygma of the Bible, is with the poor. That kerygma belongs to them "preferentially"—first and foremost. How comes it, then, that this book was so long "possessed," controlled, explained, interpreted, only by representatives of a dominant stratum of society (church hierarchy, professional theologians and exegetes, the educated)? What right is invested in them, that they can proclaim themselves *the* interpreters of the Bible? Must those who suffer wait for the affluent to explain to them the *meaning* of the liberation message of the word of God? The question of the appropriation of meaning is not irrelevant here.

By contrast, the lowly of the earth are on a "horizon of understanding" that renders the biblical kerygma "pertinent" to them. The "horizon of production" corresponds to it. There must be a common frame of reference between the sender of a message and its receiver. To give a biblical example: it would have made no sense whatever for the "oracles upon the nations" (e.g., Amos 1:3–2:5; Isa. 13–23; Jer. 46–51; Ezek. 25–32) to have been proclaimed to the nations actually cited in the text. They would have carried no "sense," no meaning, for an Egyptian or Babylonian. Rather, what we have here are messages addressed *to Israel*, in a specific literary medium, which portrays the destiny of this people in the midst of other nations. As spoken to Israel, these discourses have "pertinency"—they are on a coherent horizon of understanding. The same thing occurs on another level with the Bible in its totality. Its kerygma is most appropriate for hearing and deep understanding on the part of the deprived of this world.

This understanding of the Bible on the part of a poor people, the lowly, the suffering, sinners, and the marginalized, as their book (it "belongs" to them), and as a message concerning them first and foremost (it "pertains" to them), falls under the rubric of a totalizing reading of the Bible through its "axes of meaning," which it offers in its condition as *single text*, or extended account. It is not rare to hear from grass-roots persons in touch with real life such expressions as "We have enough of the Bible." This is not an expression of contempt, or of biblical saturation. Its meaning is that a rereading of the Bible from a point of departure in life allows for a sufficiently clear grasp of its message as pertinent, and that now what is needed is to concretize this message in action. The expression is a felicitous one, then, for it makes us realize that understanding the Bible does not require expertise, but the grasp of great lines of meaning. It suggests a reading of the Bible as a *single text*, whose meaning is now simplified vis-à-vis the plethora of little accounts composing it.

Our reading of the Bible in our Christian education and upbringing, in liturgy and preaching, in seminaries and theology departments, is a piecemeal fragmentation of a single text, rendering it a multitude of texts, leaving us with a "heap" of different meanings. Doubtless these meanings are valuable. But they sidetrack our understanding of the totalizing meaning, our understanding of the "axis" of which I have been speaking, which is more easily identified by grass-roots Christians.

Every practice or praxis constitutes a horizon of understanding for the reading of a message—in this case, that of the Bible. The hermeneutic process analyzed in chapter 1 is situated on the linguistic level—the conditions of an account as structure and totality. The treatment in chapter 2 is on the level of praxis. These are not two parallel lines prolonged indefinitely, but mutual conditions, with the decisive point in the second. In other words, *what* really generates the rereading of the Bible, and gives it its orientation, are successive practices. These cause the meaning of the texts to "enlarge"; then this meaning is expressed in new texts, which in turn condition new practices—and so on, in a progressive, enriching movement of the hermeneutic continuum. Diagram 5 synthesizes the principal points developed thus far.

A rereading returns to the event—from which it ultimately emanates—by way of earlier readings (texts). The question arises, then: Is there a shortcut to the event? Yes and no. On the one hand, the event is subsumed in the text, and in every word that is used to read it (no shortcut). On the other hand, it is also subsumed in its "historical effects," which in turn are mediated by their interpretations (word/text). Henceforth it will be a *new praxis*, rather than the intellectual study of the texts of the past, that opens the meaning of the founding event. Is this not the key to a renewed reading of the Bible—in basic ecclesial communities, for example?

Latin American popular religion is characterized by two fundamental ambiguities. The one has to do with its entanglement in a mythological mind-set. The other derives from its crystalization in an originary experience of domination and exploitation on the part of the Europeans who introduced Christianity. Latin American faith—if faith it has been— could never have had the vigor of the faith of Israel, which was founded in a paradigmatic liberation event. From this viewpoint, only when men and women of the Latin American grass roots participate in the processes of their own liberation, as subjects of their own destiny, will they be able to re-create their popular piety, and activate their many potentials in a new dimension.

3

Exegesis and Eisegesis

By now it should be abundantly clear that the exploration of the meaning of a text is not reducible to a purely literary, academic effort. Even for scholars, a determinate praxis sets the parameters for their reading. One does not "emerge" from a text (ex-egesis, from *ex* and *hegeisthai,* "to lead, to guide") with a pure meaning, gathered from within, as a diver might swim to the surface with a piece of coral in hand, or as one might take something out of a bag or trunk. One must first "get into" the text—a matter of *eis*-egesis—with questions that are not always those of its author, from a different horizon of experience, which has significant repercussions on the *production* of meaning that constitutes a rereading. We have already seen that any reading can only be a *re*reading of the meaning of a text.

A REREADING OF THE BIBLE: PART OF ITS TOTAL MESSAGE

At this point we must recall that the *whole* Bible, as we have it today, is the result, or better, the *product,* of a long hermeneutic process, in which both levels that we have examined come into play jointly: (1) that of Israel's socio-historical praxis, lived and reflected on by successive generations in continuity with the promise of salvation and the mighty deeds of salvation; and (2) that of the "recollection" of the presence of God in the form of discourse (the linguistic aspect of revelation) in the historical accounts, the "professions of faith," and the other literary genres with which the Bible abounds, until finally appearing in distinct collections—legal, prophetical, sapiential, historical, liturgical—and ultimately in the canonical text. Neither God's revelation (in events rather than in words) nor inspiration (in texts rather than in authors) is isolated phenomenon. Rather they complement and re-create each other dialectically. The "word of God" is generated in the salvific event, and interpreted and enriched by the word that "houses" it and transmits it in the form (or forms) of a message. The correlation between the "historical effect" (of an event) and the "meaning effect" (of a text) is a very intimate one, and extends to the relationship between praxis and the reading of a tradition, a text—in our case, the Bible.

Critical exegesis seeks to understand the production of texts, whereas the theological reading done from within a faith experience concentrates on the text produced, exploring its reservoir of meaning as linguistic phenomenon and as word of God. But critical exegesis is also practiced *from within a particular* (social or theological) *locus*—that is, from within a given (pre)conception of reality. Hence all *exegesis* is also *eisegesis*. A "faith-full" theological rereading, for its part, is conditioned by the structure, codes, and polysemy *of the text* (and not by some random polysemy!), which it must tirelessly explore. In this case, then, *eisegesis* is *exegesis*. The two are inseparable in the act of the production of meaning that constitutes a reading. Every reading is a hermeneutic act, whether it is a reading of the Bible or of any other sacred or nonsacred text.

It is important to recognize this. When a political reading of the Bible (which is not the only reading) on the part of the theology of liberation is criticized, the critic is making an option that is itself political (from a determinate praxis with political repercussions) and hermeneutic. The critic is seeking to "closure" a reading because its space is taken by another reading of the same genus (the political) but with a different content. Thus the reading made from within the popular church is suspected of being political, or at least sociological. But, is not the traditional, imposed reading sociological and political? And how may one ignore the fact that the Bible is a "produced" text, in hermeneutic correlation with the socio-historical reality of a whole people, and by that very fact saturated with the "political"? After all, it is the word of God for a people seeking to actualize a *historical* undertaking of peace, justice, fidelity and love, welfare and liberty.

As observed in chapter 2, an event generates an interpreting "word," and—on the "return trip," as it were—is transformed into a *founding* event, upon being charged with meaning by successive readings (see Diagram 4). And it is on the level of practices that these same readings are contextualized—where they seek to "enter" into the word-as-tradition (the text in its semiotic and hermeneutic meaning) and therefore are *eis*egetical (see Diagram 5). This phenomenon explains the formation of the Old Testament in Israel's great faith experience, as well as that of the New as a rereading of the Old (and not as a parallel body of literature) in the life of the early Christian community.

This hermeneutic process is *part of the very message of the Bible*. That is to say, the Bible, taken as "product" of a hermeneutic process, favors us with an important reading key: that its kerygmatic meaning is bestowed only in the prolongation of the same hermeneutic process (the "two-way street" from event to word and back) that has constituted the Bible. Thus, to lay claim to "fixing" its meaning once and for all at the moment of its production is to deny its *open meaning*. When, by contrast, the Bible is read from out of socio-historical reality—political, economic, cultural, religious, and the like—it reveals dimensions not previously seen, helped by beams of light not captured in earlier readings. What is unsaid in what a text "says" is said in a contextualized interpretation. This is the heart of the hermeneutic act, and a synthesis, as it were, of the results of my analysis up to this point.

UPDATING THE BIBLE? ILLUMINATION OF REALITY?

Certain notions remain to be refined. First, what I have been talking about is more than an "updating" of the biblical message, and much more than an "illumination" of our historical reality, in all the many manifestations of that reality. Consider the disjunctive nature of these so manipulated terms, which, for that matter, fail to introduce one into the heart of the hermeneutic phenomenon, or at least to explain it in its totality.

1) What is meant by "updating" or "actualizing" the biblical message? Does this mean to express it in new terms? Does it mean using popular language, changing Semitic idioms to idioms closer to our own, circumlocuting pregnant, but culturally contextualized, expressions with explanatory glosses? This last is what popular versions of the Bible often do. The advantages are undeniable, provided one is aware that these semantic modernizations are a matter of temporary usefulness and cannot be expected to last long (the problem with a popular version of the Bible that becomes traditional). Actually, the forms of "updating" just mentioned are really only "translation," and as such, although they enter into the realm of hermeneutics, they do not always reach its heart.

Or does "updating the Bible" mean rendering the biblical kerygma *effective* for our de facto situations? Surely it must mean this, whatever else it may also mean. But how does a message expressed in another age, for a people of another cultural and social milieu, become effective in our time and place? Clearly, this is a demand for "doing something" with the *text* in which the message is inscribed. It is by applying the laws of the linguistics of discourse (chapter 1), and by recalling the process of the event-become-word (chapter 2), that a meaning unfolds in the biblical text—a meaning that overflows its first referent. In this same way a message is discovered that was not exhausted in its first actualization. Thus we emerge upon a *newness* of meaning, characteristic of any hermeneutic reading, and particularly evident in all religious traditions. A simple linguistic "updating" of the kerygma does not have this scope, although it tends in the right direction. After all, is there no novelty in the christological rereading of the Old Testament practiced in the apostolic age and reflected in the books of the New Testament? How, then, can our own interpretation of the Bible, done in the framework of new historical and faith experiences, be anything but new?

We must *re-create* the message of the Bible, not just "update" it. This is neither preposterous nor unexemplified. Creative rereading of the Bible is already being done from within the popular church, out of pioneer historical processes, out of cultural and religious contexts different from those of the Semitic or Western worlds, by theologians who are listening to, if not (more likely) immersed in, the life of the people.

2) What I have just pointed out clarifies in turn the notion of the "illumination" of the history, the reality, of Third World peoples, from a point of departure in the Bible understood as the word of God. There is not one route only, emerging only *from* the biblical text. Hermeneutic circularity implies a "return trip," as a complement of the earlier, in view of the fact that the praxis of faith in a determinate social context also has a contribution to make to the "meaning" of the Bible, opening it up precisely as "word of God."

For example, does not an evaluation, from within, of the religions and cultures of Asia, Africa, and Latin America have something to contribute to our understanding of the many biblical texts expressing contempt for the religious symbols of Israel's neighbors? Does not the cry of oppressed groups and classes cry out against an excessively "spiritualized," eschatologizing interpretation of the New Testament?

CLOSED OR OPEN REVELATION?

Does all this perhaps mean "adding to" or "subtracting from" the word of God? Clearly, I collide here with the theologoumenon of a revelation closed, closured, with Christ, with the last Apostle, or with the last book of the New Testament, depending on the version of the theory.

To begin with, these three postulated closures are not synonymous. The first—revelation completed in Christ—implies a qualitative criterion, the second a temporal boundary, and the third a textual and linguistic limit. But they explain one another. Christ is the acme and crown of revelation, but the canonical text culminating in the Book of Revelation gathers up the post-Paschal, apostolic experience of the primordial Christian community. The extension of revelation is limited, then, to the life of Israel and the lifetime of the apostles, the witnesses of Jesus' ministry, death, and resurrection.

This is correct, as far as it goes. But it does not go far enough. Indeed Christ is the crowning point, the highest point, of God's manifestation in salvation history. But was there no divine self-manifestation before (and before Israel!) or since? Or does "revelation" mean only uttering words? This is the direction the problem moves in, and the explanation will be—of course—hermeneutic: the event is gathered up in the word-as-account, and the word-as-account then begins to circulate as message or meaning *of the* (first) *event,* as linguistic meaning or message. This phenomenon, which we have already analyzed, is most significant, and constitutes the matrix of the hermeneutic process. The event has "meaning" insofar as it is interpreted. Afterward, the vehicle of meaning is a *text* (written or oral; and finally written). Until, in a hermeneutic option, a text is taken up into a "canon" that closures other traditions, it is fatuous to claim that it can closure its own rereading and be considered a "deposit" of revelation.[38]

Just as an event can become a "founding" event in light of its historical effects, so also a text becomes normative and archetypal within a community that lives in its atmosphere. A canon becomes necessary only when a conflict of opinions becomes so intense that division results. New groups must recompose or restate a text of reference—in the religious sphere, a "canon of sacred scripture." That the Bible is our paradigmatic text as the word of God, therefore, as our faith asserts, is tremendously important. We have no need of new books to add to the Bible; Christian practices are definitively orientated by those of Jesus and his teaching (interpreted, to be sure, in a canonical *text*).

But this is not the end of the matter (as if a hermeneutic process could come to an end!). One of the "semantic axes" of the Bible is precisely that God is primarily revealed *in the events* of human history. This presence, seized by faith, simultaneously generates faith, inasmuch as the latter, initially, as the Bible recounts, is a "grateful acknowledgment" of the presence of God in human occurrences. Faith as adherence to a word or a person is a hermeneutic "after." Every element of the event that is gathered in the word—and this is a key point of hermeneutics, especially biblical hermeneutics—has to do with this "grateful acknowledgment" sort of faith in God. Before God's self-manifestation in word there is God's self-manifestation in salvific deeds and their consequences—the "historical effects" that prolong this same epiphany. The expression of God's revelation in a word, in a text, is also an "after." Even the biblical word of the "promise" is mediated by a text orientating it to the exodus occurrence *supposed as experienced,* so that the text is itself a kind of rereading of the occurrence. Paradoxically, the promise—as a text that we read today—is a theological development from a point of departure in the occurrence it announces! The *accounts* of the call of the prophets (e.g., Amos 7:10–17; Isa. 6; Jer. 1; Ezek. 1–3) come only after the activity of the respective prophets. (The *account* comes later, not the call.) This is a rereading of the prophet's message according to the tradition retransmitting the message.

Let us return to the question of the terminus of revelation. When a prophet of Israel speaks in God's name (and cites God's "word"), the prophet is "reading" or hearing it *in the life of the people,* in the infidelity or suffering of the people. The prophet codes God's word as judgment or as promise of salvation. God is in the *event,* and the prophet translates this divine presence-in-life into a "word."

And if "the Word became flesh" (John 1:14), does that not gainsay all intent to closure the word of God in the Torah, the law? The Torah, reflection and multiform expression of God's revelation in history, has its meaning threatened if totalized as an autonomous word—closed, impermeable to new manifestations of God that would modify its readings now (seemingly!) fixed in tradition. Christ was God's *new* event that imperated a *rereading* of the Torah.

Unable to recognize, to "acknowledge," God in Jesus' practices and words, many Jews of his time, unbeknown to themselves, lost their status as "God-experts." "If you knew me, you would know my father too" (John 8:19)—once more, (re)cognition, grateful acknowledgment, of God in human occurrences (here, in Jesus). "Whoever looks on me is seeing him who sent me" (John 12:45; cf. 14:7). It is most arresting that Jesus could say—in the Johannine account—that the "theologians" of that time, the "God-knowers," had suddenly been transformed into "God-unknowers."

God bestowed a self-epiphany in the historical Jesus. It was a "matter of faith" to identify God there. But is the closure of God in the Torah a "matter of faith"? Is God in a text—or in life? Surely there is a conflict of interpretations here. But there is also reductionism of revelation. Such was the drama of the Jews who allowed the God-event in Jesus to "get by them," instead of seizing it and making it their starting point for a rereading of the scriptures that had been handed down as the "word" of God.

The cycle is repeated in the history of the church. The theologoumenon of a "closed revelation," a revelation over and done, in spite of all its good intentions, and indeed all the truth it contains as a symbolic expression, produces a "short circuit" in the revelation process itself. It seeks to move directly from God to word, instead of God to event to word.

But are we to be left with nothing more than a *word* to "illuminate" human events, the vicissitudes of a people or peoples? Is God saying nothing *new* in the struggles of the oppressed, in the processes of liberation, in the contribution of the human sciences to a deeper knowledge of humankind and its problems, to a knowlege of reality and its oppressive structures, to a knowledge of human creative capacities in their thrust to build a new humankind in a new society? There is more here than just a novelty in the order of knowledge of revelation already made, and more than just the fact that God is manifested in modalities not previously known or experienced (by plumbing earlier revelation—ultimately, then, a matter of deepening knowledge of what is already known). What is crucial is that God's self-revelation to us takes place in *events*.

If this is the case, then this epiphany on the part of God ought to generate a hermeneutic process that will produce its own word: the faith discourse in all its modulations—prayer, creed, proclamation, theology—a genuinely new word. It ought to produce not an "illumination" of present history by a kind of light shining on it from behind (the biblical text), but a grasp of God's face as sketched in the history of men and women. The Bible itself orientates our reading of God *in the events* of the world, and teaches us, precisely, to recognize God *in present self-revelations,* and not as a repetition of the past. Human history is constant novelty, and so is the presence of God accompanying it.

Christ, as central, crowning event of history, is an unfinished event. Christian apocalyptic awaits him a second time to "close" this history. The Jewish response to the Christian acknowledgment of Jesus as the Messiah and the savior is that "the world is still the same." This reasoning is based on a conception according to which Christ (were he the Messiah) would be the *telos* of revelation and of God's salvific activity. All would have been said, all would have been done, and it would remain only to explicitate and deepen what has been said, and produce the effects of what has been done, in subsequent history.

But is it not more in conformity with the New Testament to assert that eschatology and the new order *begin* with Christ, that he is a hermeneutic key for the discovery of God in our history? John 1:18 says, magnificently, that the Logos-Word has *exegesato* the Father—has made known, "exegeted," the Father. But Christ has not said all. He left us his Spirit, to teach us (John 14:26) and "lead [us] to all truth" (*hodegesei humans eis ten aletheian pasan;* John 16:13). The Bible is the faith reading of paradigmatic occurrences of salvific history, and a paradigmatic reading of a salvation history that is not yet over.

The Bible as paradigmatic, normative message does not preclude its own rereading in the light of new events. As it is meaningless (because it is opposed to the very form of the biblical message) to closure God's revelation in past history, so is it meaningless to transform the Bible into a closured "deposit," from which one need only "pull things out." As normative, canonical text of God's salvific message, and precisely as normative, it incorporates—by virtue of its rereading—the *new* meaning of new events of history.

*Interpretation is accumulation of meaning. Ex*egesis is *eis*egesis—"entering into" the biblical text, with a cargo of meaning that re-creates the first meaning precisely because it is placed in harmony with it, whether by virtue of the continuum of a faith praxis (on the level of "historical effect"), or by virtue of the continuum of successive interpretations or re-readings (on the level of hermeneutic tradition).

This decisive quality of event—of history—as prime locus

of God's revelation, yesterday and today, demonstrates how feeble, how crippled, any theology will be when it is founded solely on the transmitted source(s) of revelation. Whether the foundation be *scriptura sola* or scripture-and-tradition makes little difference. If tradition is living, it will "dovetail" with what I call God's *ongoing* revelation in history. But the Catholic view of tradition transforms it from a deed into a *text* (the writings of the fathers of the church, liturgical texts, and so on), thus extending biblical revelation a short distance, but still closures it at some point, subjecting it to the control of a magisterial authority. Henceforth we are once more in a "theology of fonts." There is no epistemological difference between that theology and a "theology of the Torah" inasmuch as both channel God's entire revelation through vessels already full, capped, and stored in a "deposit."

By contrast, how difficult an "open theology" is! No wonder that the theology coming to life in Latin America is conflictual. The same thing happens with the new language about God (that is, theology) arising from a faith practice among committed Christians elsewhere. The only legitimate function of a church magisterium (in Catholicism) or a confessional tradition (in Protestantism) will be to unify and *momentarily* closure the meaning of a tradition or a praxis—while making way for a new opening, in the light of the alternation between praxis and text that constitutes the hermeneutic process. What is not biblical, and not hermeneutic, is the total closure of *one* reading of the kerygma, or its purely authoritarian control.

THE LANGUAGE OF FAITH

It is important to notice that God's revelation in events, and not only in transmitted words, helps us to an in-depth understanding of biblical tradition. The language of the Bible shares the characteristics of all religious language: in literary symbols and narrative codes it expresses the *meaning* that *faith* discovers in human occurrences having at first blush nothing extraordinary about them. The *event* of the deliverance from slavery in Egypt was the same for the Egyptians and for the Hebrews, and could have taken place among Canaanite or Libyan slaves of the time. By contrast, the *representation* of an event such as that of the "crossing of the sea," in any of the accounts that proclaim and describe it, forms part of the "word"-of-the-event, the word that bespeaks the presence of God acting in history, in a liberation process.

This has three important consequences.

1) The salvific event is better "centered." It is the experience of *liberation,* and not simply the crossing of the sea or the coming of a plague. These representations *interpret* the event; they do not simply repeat it.

2) The *text* or account interpreting and amplifying the kerygmatic and theological dimensions of the deed of liberation is seen in its proper light. Once it is "read" in a "word," the event is subsumed in that word, and its "historical effects" (the practices it generates) will then be subsumed in it as well, in a dialectical, meaning-creating sequence. The text, then, is the vehicle of a message because it continually incorporates its own rereading, called for by practice and by the work of faith, which continues to discover the ever new God of history.

3) *Faith* is decisive for the formulation and profession of the salvific presence of God in human deeds. To think that God's self-manifestation must take place in miracles and extraordinary phenomena, as the *account* of the exodus, and so many others, relate, is to fall victim to the naivety of those who are ignorant of how religious discourse is initiated. Religious discourse is an "afterward" with respect to the event. It is the reading of the event. Are not the liberation of Nicaragua or of African peoples today salvific events, and, from a Christian viewpoint, manifestations *of God?* To think of them as human political events (which they are), *and* thereupon to make the *theological* assertion that God is not revealed in them, is to be satisfied with a revelation "on deposit," and to

repeat the altogether *hermeneutical* attitude of the Pharisees, who characterized the Jesus event as "demoniacal" (Luke 11:15, 19).

Traditional theology has fostered the belief that the biblical kerygma is expressed in concepts. But it is quite adept at speaking of symbols (improperly referred to as "signs") in its discourse upon the sacraments. It fails to grasp that God can be spoken of only in *symbols* (natural things transparently referring to a second meaning, which somehow transcends phenomenal experience) or *myth* (combinations of symbols built into an account of origins, in order to express the meaning of some present reality, institution, custom, or the like). The faith of Israel established a breach with the mythical worldview—the fragmentation of the sacred into phenomena of nature (hence its cyclic schema), but never with the *language* of myth, that indispensable form of religious discourse. The symbol, by virtue of its semantic polysemy, refers to another sphere. Myth is a "broken" language, elaborating a "history" of marvelous happenings in the divine world that inaugurate the present order. Its purpose is to "bespeak" the transcendent, or simply the deeper level of meaning resident in things, for what is relevant in the life of the human being inserted into a group. (A myth is always held in community.)

In a word, language about God cannot abstract from *images*. God cannot be conceptualized. Dogma is a form of *gnosis,* which pares the faith experience down to rational dimensions of interpretation.[39] God is represented in images. And the Bible, every step of the way, is a *representation* of God, whether in the language of symbol and myth (even the most "historical" accounts are interpreted and "broken" in order to express a faith dimension), or in that of the many linguistic codes or literary genres that are another expression of the "image" (in the sense that each genre communicates a message by its linguistic structure and not only by its content—through "form," and not only through concepts).

RECONTEXTUALIZATION OF THE BIBLICAL KERYGMA

Revelation is a challenge, driving us to discover in an event a wealth of meaning that need not necessarily "coincide" with what occurred in Israel. But the language of faith, because of this very wealth, is conditioned in two ways.

1) First, it starts with an experience or an event that is per se fleeting and irreversible. The discourse of faith continually shifts, contemplating that event from within new experiences or practices. This is the distance that draws out the reservoir of meaning of the event, or of the account that has already read the event. Strange, then, the boundless preoccupation with the immobilization of dogma. There is no point in denying it: dogmas have a closuring function at a determinate moment in the theological discussion of the interpretation of praxis. This is a way in which the community defends its identity. The antihermeneutic element here is the petrification of dogma in definitive formulas.

2) At the same time, the language of faith is necessarily limited—culturally and literally. This is a condition of all language. All discourse—as the attempt to "say something to someone about something"—requires a *contextual* closure to render it intelligible. Otherwise it is not a *message*. There are, after all, no universal languages. Nor has the Bible been written somewhere up in the stratosphere, wafting above times and cultures. It was written by and for the Hebrew people. Only by way of profound rereadings did it come to be the book of the first Christians, in a restricted geographical area. This means that the biblical message is heavily contextualized. In order to be understood from within other historical situations, it must now be *re*contextualized. If the Christian can read the signs of the times, this reading will be in harmony with the "kerygmatic axes" of the Bible, themselves coded in the "semantic axes"

(on the textual level) that have been treated above.

This hermeneutic perspective—reinforced by recourse to semiotics—guarantees the legitimacy of grass-roots theologies such as the theology of liberation. That this theology begins with a correct and conscientized analysis of social reality does not make it sociology or anthropology. Is it of no importance to *know* the reality in which *God* is epiphanized? Cannot the social sciences be utilized as instruments for recontextualizing the message of God? It is faith, of course, that thereupon recognizes, in situations of captivity, marginalization, or oppression—and in every human situation—God's call to full realization.

SOME OBJECTIONS

Emphasis on the recontextualization of the Bible—in a theology of liberation, in base-level church communities, by Christians committed to social change, and the like—occasions some objections.

1) The reading of the Bible would appear to become *subjective,* with little foundation in the Bible itself, paradoxically. But I think that what happens is just the opposite. The imputation of "subjectivity" lodged against biblical hermeneutics would in that case be valid with respect to all theology, inasmuch as there is no such thing as an "objective" theology. Not even an academic exegesis can be such.

The "semiotic recourse," as we have seen, demonstrates that the hermeneutics of a text is conditioned *by the text itself.* The text indicates the limit (however broad) of its own meaning. Textual polysemy does not mean simply what-you-will. *A text says what it permits to be said.* Its polysemy arises from its previous *closure.* Hence the urgency of situating it in its proper context, by means of historico-critical methods, and of exploring its capacity for the production of meaning (according to the laws of semiotics), in order thus to cause its "forward" to blossom from within life.

2) It is likewise commonplace to hear all committed theology, especially Latin American, criticized for "using the Old Testament more than the New." Now, first of all, the whole Bible is the word of God, and one has the right to use the Old Testament as much as one may wish. But secondly, the Bible is a *single* text, the continuous presentation of a soteriological project that passes by way of determinate narrative and kerygmatic axes. Thirdly, the Old Testament contains a more extensive narrative theology than the New Testament, furnishing numerous examples of historical occurrences seen in the light of the founding event of the exodus. Fourthly, no one can deny that the Bible is supremely varied and rich with respect to theological currents. Hence the importance of taking it as one great account.

Further: there is a hermeneutic principle, flowing from the analysis that we have made, according to which the kerygma is not lost when reread on a deeper level, but capable of being resumed repeatedly. The fact that the Old Testament is reread in the New does not mean that the Old Testament must be abrogated or "shelved." The "hermeneutic fecundation" effectuated by such rereading is only further motivation for sounding the depths of its inexhaustible meaning.

In fact, some readings of the "Christic fact" gathered up in the New Testament itself quite pass over important kerygmatic elements in the Old: individual sin, for example, is much more prominent in the New Testament than are social structures (contrast the prophets of Israel). The eschatologization of the kingdom of God (but not in Luke!) seems to relativize the struggle for a just order in this world. Paul contemplates slavery from such heights that he loses his concern for the real situation of the actual slave (1 Cor. 7:20–24; 1 Tim. 6:1–2), and excludes women from the word in church assemblies (1 Cor. 14:34–35; cf. 11:2–15). He recommends obedience on the part of Roman Christians to the authorities of the oppressive Roman empire (Rom. 13:1–7).

Any text, in the intention of its author, is a closure of

meaning. Furthermore, the author's meaning is contextual and "conjunctural." But the author "dies" in the transmission of the text, and its polysemy emerges. This entails a risk and an advantage. The risk is precisely in the decontextualization implied in a subsequent reading of the text. Let us take the case of 1 Corinthians 14:33b–35. In writing to a Greek church, surely Paul may not have considered it opportune suddenly to negate a cultural praxis, doubtless based on an Orphico-Platonic worldview, that idealized men and scorned women. A decontextualized universalization of this text elevates to a "doctrine" what may have been a circumstantial indication. This would save Paul—but not the text! And we do not read *Paul* today, but the *text* he wrote!

And what is the advantage of passing from author to text? At the linguistic level this account is within another account— the Bible as a totality. (Recall the concept of intratextuality.) In this single text, we have another Pauline affirmation: "There does not exist among you . . . male or female. All are one in Christ Jesus. Furthermore, if you belong to Christ . . . you inherit all that was promised" (Gal. 3:28–29). This time we have a more radical principle, subsuming the other and "referring" it definitively to the Old Testament (Gen. 1:26; cf. Eph. 5:31–32). In the recirculation established in this intratextuality (if not indeed in the very intertextuality) of the Bible, the Old Testament has not lost its meaning, because it is being read through a christological prism. Thus there is no question of any abuse of the Old Testament.

CONCLUSION

The Bible is our "word of God." It is the recollection and regathering of the meaning of God's salvific deeds. It is not only a text to be read, it is also a word proclaimed, which reinterprets the text, for life. We have seen that, just as event becomes word, and word emerges in text, so text, in turn, calls for a new word, to reread it. Thus we have a sequential rotation, in which the word generates the text and the text generates the word.

This relationship likewise obtains between sacred scripture as a totality and the word proclaiming the kerygma. Scripture was proclamation before, and is proclamation after. Christ, too, is Word interpreted by the (Old Testament) scriptures, but then he is interpreted in new texts forming the New Testament. And so we come to new scriptures, which in their turn are summed up in proclamation. Thus scripture becomes word, word becomes scripture. The movement can never come to an end. For behind it is the presence of God in life—a God of the living, and not of the dead (Matt. 22:32).[40]

Notes

1. *Liberación y libertad. Pautas hermenéuticas* (Buenos Aires, Mundo Nuevo, 1973; Lima, CEP, 1978); Engl. trans., *Exodus: A Hermeneutics of Freedom* (Maryknoll, N.Y., Orbis, 1981).

2. "La tarea de la hermenéutica," in *Exégesis: Problemas de método y ejercicios de lectura* (Buenos Aires, La Aurora, 1978) 219; emphasis added.

3. Ricoeur, "Hermenéutica filosófica y hermenéutica bíblica," ibid., 263–77 (see p. 263s).

4. Croatto, *Exodus*, 2.

5. See K. Otte, *Das Sprachverständnis bei Philo von Alexandrien. Sprache als Mittel der Hermeneutik* (Tübingen, Mohr, 1968); I. Christiansen, *Die Technik der allegorischen Auslegungswissenschaft bei Philo von Alexandrien* (Tübingen, Mohr, 1969).

6. See A. Díez Macho, *"Deras* y exégesis del Nuevo Testamento," *Sefarad,* 35 (1975) 37–89; idem, *El Targum: Introducción a las traducciones aramaicas de la Biblia* (Madrid, SCIC, 2nd ed., 1979).

7. For an overview of this problem, see Ricoeur, "La tarea," 221ff.

8. See B. S. Childs, "The *sensus litteralis* of Scripture," in *Beiträge zur alttestamentlichen Theologie: Festschrift W. Zimmerli* (Göttingen, Vandenhoeck & Ruprecht, 1977) 80–93, esp. 88ff.

9. See C. E. Braaten, *History and Hermeneutics* (London, Lutterworth, 1968), chap. 6; H. Kimmerle, "Hermeneutical Theory or Ontological Hermeneutics," in *History and Hermeneutic* (New York, Harper & Row, 1967) 107–21; J. M. Robinson and E. Fuchs, *La nuova ermeneutica* (Brescia, Paideia, 1967).

10. What some call the "ontological (-historical) parameter." See R. Lapointe, *Les trois dimensions de l'herméneutique* (Paris, Gabalda, 1967) 89ff.

11. This is a very remarkable fact in narrative semiotics, analyzed in detail by all those who investigate the structural analysis of accounts (R. Barthes, T. Todorov, J. Kristeva, and others). In the case of the Bible, see, e.g., J. Calloud, *Structural Analysis of Narrative* (Philadelphia, Fortress, 1976).

12. Ricoeur, "Evénement et sens," *Archivio di Filosofia* (1971) 15–34;

idem, "La función hermenéutica de la distanciación," in *Exégesis* (n. 2, above) esp. 247ff.

13. See J. L. Austin, *How to Do Things with Words* (Harvard University Press, 1975); J. R. Searle, *An Essay in the Philosophy of Language* (Cambridge University Press, 1969).

14. The author of the Book of Sirach (Ecclesiasticus), according to the Greek (LXX) text, is "Jesus, the son of Eleazar, son of Sirach" (50:27), whereas the (noncanonical) Hebrew text identifies him as the son of Simeon. This twofold tradition is not without significance.

15. For these terms, see Grupo de Entrevernes, *Análisis semiótico de los textos. Introducción—Teoría—Práctica* (Madrid, Cristiandad, 1982); idem, *Signos y parábolas. Semiótica y texto evangélico* (Madrid, Cristiandad, 1979); *Iniciación en el análisis estructural* (Estella, Verbo Divino, 1980).

16. *Signos y parábolas,* 236.

17. In the canonical structure of the fourth Gospel, chapters 1–2 find their counterpart in chapters 20–21.

18. See P. Grelot, *Les poèmes du Serviteur. De la lecture critique à l'herméneutique* (Paris, Cerf, 1981) 67–73.

19. E.g., Isa. 49:6b (LXX) reads: "I will make you a light to the nations, *so that you may be* salvation to the ends of the earth" (the words in italic are a deviation from the Hebrew, profoundly modifying its meaning). See Grelot, *Les poèmes,* 82ff.

20. A listing of these passages, with a commentary in the light of the Hebrew text, is found in Grelot, *Les poèmes,* 138–89. He finds reminiscenses, imitations, and direct quotations of the Servant songs in Paul, Hebrews, 1 Peter, Luke/Acts, Matthew, John, and (probably) Mark.

21. See R. Pietrantonio, "El Mesías asesinado. El Mesías ben Efraim en el evangelio de Juan," *Revista Bíblica,* 44/1/5 (1982) 1–64.

22. Compare Isa. 50:4–5 in the Hebrew and targumic texts:

Hebrew	*Targum*
The Lord God has given me the tongue of a teacher so that I may know how to speak a reassuring word to the weary. Morning after morning he opens my ear to listen as one trained. The Lord God has opened my ear [lament of the persecuted *Servant*].	Yahweh-God has given me the tongue of those who teach, in order to know how to teach the righteous, who languish for the words of his law, wisdom. Thus, early every morning, he sends his prophets in case that the ears of sinners be open and that they would accept his teach-

ing. Yahweh-God has sent
me to prophesy [lament of
the persecuted *prophet*].

Only a few words of the older text are found here! The targumic text is, in reality, a metatext.

Isa. 53:10, so decisive in the christological rereading of the New Testament, in the targum completely loses its original appearance:

Hebrew	*Targum*
The Lord God was pleased to crush him with sorrows. If he gives himself in expiation, he will see descendants, he will prolong his days, and he will do the will of the Lord by his hand.	The Lord God was pleased to perfect and purify the remnant of his people, in order to purge their souls of their sins; they will see the reign of his messiah; their sons and daughters will multiply, and they will prolong their days; and those who do the will of Yahweh will prosper according to his good will.

23. A targum is an (interpretive) translation or paraphrase of the Hebrew into the Aramaic. A midrash is an amplification of a text or passage in the direction of a new account. Both follow hermeneutical norms, but the midrash has greater possibilities for expanding—and hence actualizing—a text. See R. Le Déaut, "Un phénomène spontané de l'herméneutique juive ancienne: le 'targumisme,' " *Bíblica,* 52 (1971) 505–25; idem, "La tradition juive ancienne et l'éxègese chrétienne primitive," *Revue d'Histoire et de Philosophie Religieuses,* 51 (1971) 31–50; E. Levine, "La evolución de la Biblia aramea," *Estudios Bíblicos,* 39 (1981) 223–48; Díez Macho, *El Targum* (n. 6, above).

24. It is not surprising, then, that H. M. Orlinsky denies the basis for a christological reading of Isa. 53: "The So-Called 'Suffering Servant' in Isaiah 53," in *Interpreting the Prophetic Tradition* (New York, KTAV, 1969) 25–73; idem, "The So-Called 'Servant of the Lord' " and " 'Suffering Servant' in Second Isaiah," in N. H. Snaith, ed., *Studies on the Second Part of the Book of Isaiah* (Leiden, Brill, 1967) 66ff., esp. 73 and 118 (Orlinsky subscribes to the basic principle of hermeneutical eisegesis!).

25. On the theme of the underground communication of myths irreducible to one another, which I here validate for *all* events and texts, see

Ricoeur, *La simbólica del mal* (vol. 2 of *Finitud y Culpabilidad*) (Madrid, Taurus, 1969) 649ff. (Eng. trans, *The Symbolism of Evil* [New York: Harper & Row, 1967].

26. See Ricoeur, "La función hermenéutica" (n. 12, above).

27. See H.G. Gadamer, *Verdad y método. Fundamentos de una hermenéutica filosófica* (Salamanca, Sígume, 1977) 370ff. (Engl. trans., *Truth and Method* [New York, Seabury, 1975]).

28. I cite only texts from the Book of Isaiah, because they are especially prominent there. There have been many studies on the theme of the "new exodus" in Isaiah, especially Deutero-Isaiah. See, e. g., Carroll Stuhlmueller, *Creative Redemption in Deutero-Isaiah* (Rome, Pontifical Biblical Institute, 1970); J. Blenkinsopp, "Objetivo y profundidad de la tradición del éxodo en Déutero-Isaías 40-55," *Concilium* (Dec. 1966) 397–407; K. Keisov, *Exodustexte im Jesajabuch. Literarkritische und motivgeschichtliche Analysen* (Freiburg, Orbis Biblicus et Orientalis, 1979). H. Simián, relying mostly on extratextual arguments, denies the presence of this theme in Deutero-Isaiah: "Exodo en Deuteroisaías," *Bíblica*, 61 (1980) 530–53.

29. On the meaning of "knowledge of mystery" that includes *pesher* (a hermeneutical aspect), see F. García Martínez, "El pesher: interpretación profética de la Escritura," *Salmanticensis*, 26 (1979) 125–39.

30. See n. 6, above.

31. See "Yavé, el Dios de la 'presencia' salvífica. Ex. 3, 14 en su contexto literario y querigmático," *Revista Bíblica*, 43/3/3 (1981) 153–63; "Yo estaré (contigo). Interpretación de Ex. 3, 13–14," in V. Collado and E. Zurro, eds., *El misterio de la palabra* (Madrid, Cristiandad, 1983) 147–59.

32. See H. H. Schmid, *Gerechtigkeit als Weltordnung* (Tübingen, Mohr, 1968); A. Gamper, *Gott als Richter in Mesopotamien und in Alten Testament* (Innsbruck, Wagner, 1966). These themes appear especially in legal documents and royal titles; see S. H. Paul, *Studies in the Book of the Covenant in the Light of Cuneiform and Biblical Law* (Leiden, Brill, 1970); M. J. Seux, *Epithètes royales akkadiennes et sumériennes* (Paris, Letouzey et Ané, 1967); N. P. Lemche, *"Anduràrum* and *misarum:* Comments on the Problem of Social Edicts and their Applications in the Ancient Near East," *Journal of Near Eastern Studies,* 38 (1979) 11–22; H. J. Boecker, *Law and the Administration of Justice in the Old Testament and Ancient East* (Minneapolis, Augsburg, 1980). I have made a synthesis of this thematic in "El Mesías liberador de los pobres," *Revista Bíblica,* 32/137 (1970) 233–40.

33. A good exegetical reading of Luke 4 is that by C. Escudero Freire, *Devolver el Evangelio a los pobres* (Salamanca, Sígueme, 1978) 138–41 and esp. 259–77.

34. See J. C. Maraschin, "Boas novas aos pobres e libertação aos presos e oprimidos," *Simpôsio,* 21 (1980) 36–51; J. Pixley, "El Reino de Dios, ¿buenas nuevas para los pobres?," *Cuadernos de Teología,* 4/2 (1976) 77–103; Croatto, *Exodus* (n. 1, above), chap. 5.

35. See Croatto, "Palabra profética y no-conversión: la tematizacion bíblica del rechazo al profeta' in *Vox Evangelii 1* (Buenos Aires, ISEDET, 1984) 9-20.

36. For the structuring of international sovereignty/vassalage pacts echoed in the Bible, see *Historia de la salvación* (Buenos Aires, Paulinas, 6th ed., 1983) 50ff.

37. See "Una promesa aún no cumplida. Algunos enfoques sobre la estructura del Pentateuco," *Revista Bíblica,* 44/4/8 (1982) 193-206.

38. It can be objected that the idea of a "deposit" of faith is biblical (1 Tim. 6:20; 2 Tim. 1:14). But the *text* of these two epistles intends precisely a "closure" of doctrine vis-à-vis other groups; it does not refer to the Bible (New Testament) as not yet constituted. The context is specific. The Greek word used in both texts, *paratheke,* sometimes translated "deposit" (e. g., in the NAB), can be translated otherwise. "Keep safe *what has been entrusted* to you" (1 Tim. 6:20, NEB). "Guard the *treasure* put into our charge" (2 Tim. 1:14, NEB). "Keep *what has been confided* to you" (2 Tim. 1:14, *El Libro del Pueblo de Dios. La Biblia* [Madrid/Buenos Aires, Paulinas, 1980]). This Spanish translation is less precise than others, but it avoids—intentionally—the term "deposit."

39. See Ricoeur, "Introducción a la simbólica del mal," in *El conflicto de las interpretaciones* (Buenos Aires, La Aurora, 1976), vol. 2, pp. 25ff. (Engl. trans., *The Conflict of Interpretations: Essays in Hermeneutics* [Northwestern University Press, 1974]).

40. I have condensed the contents of this book in "L'herméneutique biblique en face des méthodes critiques: défi et perspectives," in *Congress Volume. Salamanca 1983* (Suppl. to *Vetus Testamentum,* 36, Leiden, E. J. Brill, 1985) 67-80. See also "Biblical Hermeneutics in the Theologies of Liberation," in V. Fabella and S. Torres (eds.), *Irruption of the Third World. Challenge to Theology* (New York, Orbis Books, 1983) 140–68.

Glossary

Axis of Meaning or Semantic Axis. The recurring theme or motif structuring a text as a whole.

Darash. An interpretation exploring the deep, hidden meaning of a text. Distinguished from *pashat.*

Diachrony. The chronological or successive nature of a reality or text and of its signification. Distinguished from synchrony.

Eisegesis. The reader's "entry" into a text from his or her own "horizon of understanding." Not opposed to exegesis, but an explicitation of one of its aspects.

Fusion of Horizons. The mutual relationship between the horizon of the text (rather than of the author) and that of the interpreter in the act of reading.

Intertextuality. The meaning of one text in the light of others, within the same worldview. (Linguistic correlate of the "analogy of faith.") Distinguished from intratextuality.

Intratextuality. The meaning of a text in itself, with the text taken as a structured totality. Distinguished from intertextuality.

Midrash. As a method of interpretation, identical with *darash,* except that midrash deals with concrete texts. See n. 23.

Narratary. Addressee of a text not considered as an extralinguistic entity. Distinguished from (extralinguistic) addressee. The narratary is the intralinguistic receiver of the message.

Pashat. Rabbinical term for the "simple," immediate, surface meaning of a text, in the author's own context. Distinguished from *darash.*

Pertinency. Nature of a text or discourse appropriate to a particular addressee, in being germane to his or her "horizon of understanding."

Pesher. Literally, "explanation." An interpretive explanation of a text. As a literary genre, typical of the Dead Sea scrolls of Qumran, and of apocalyptic literature generally. See Daniel 7:16. See also n. 29.

Polysemy. Plurality of meanings of a text, sentence, or event.

Recontextualization. The act of referring a text to the reader's "horizon of meaning" in a rereading of that text.

15370

Referent. The extralinguistic reality to which a text refers. Distinguished from the "meaning" of the text, which is intralinguistic.

Rereading. An interpretative reading of a text "enlarging" its "originary meaning."

Reservoir of Meaning. The capacity of a text to "say" more than its author consciously intended. Textual correlate of rereading.

Semantic. Pertaining to the evolution and "enlargement" of meaning of a word or text. Distinguished from semiotic.

Semiotic. Pertaining to the analysis of the structural aspect of the meaning of a text. Distinguished from semantic.

Significate. Text as message, as what the text "says." Distinguished from signifier.

Signifier. Text as a sign or structure. Distinguished from significate.

Synchrony. The simultaneous nature of signification in the reading and interpretation of a text as a whole.

Targum. Aramaic translation of the Hebrew Bible. Interpretive, but less excursive than midrash. See n. 23.

Torah. The Pentateuch. By extension, the whole of the Jewish scriptures, as divine norm and founding institution of a community.

Scriptural Index

Genesis

1:1	23
1:5	7
1:8	7
1:13	7
1:19	7
1:23	7
1:31	7
1:26	7
22	54

Exodus

3:12-14	52

Deuteronomy

6:20-24	60
15:6	59
26:5-9	60

Joshua

3-5	37

Nehemiah

8-10	61
9:36-37	61

Psalms

78:4b-7	54
78:9	54
78:10–11	54
78:67-72	55

Isaiah

6	72
11:15-16	39
13:23	63
19:16-25	39
42:1-9	28
43:16-21	39
49:3	27
49:5-6	28
49:7	28
50:4-5	85n.22
50:4-11	28
51:9-11	39
52:13-53:12	28
53	29, 30, 32
53:4	26
53:8	26
53:10	86n.22
53:12	26
60:12	59
61:1-2	53

Jeremiah

1	72
46-51	63

Ezekiel

1-3	72
25-32	63

Amos

1:1-9	55, 56
1:1-9:10	56
1:1-9:15	56
1:3-2:25	63
1:10	55
1:11-15	55
2:6-16	56
7:10-17	72
9:11-15	56

Matthew

23:32	83

Luke

1:32	29
1:69	29
3:31	29
4:16-30	53
4:43	53
11:15-19	78
20:41-44	29
24:25-26	29
24:46	29

John

1:1	23
1:4	73
1:19	22
1:29	22
1:35-51	22, 24
1:36	23, 24
1:37	24
1:38	23, 24
1:39	23, 24
1:40	24
1:41	24
1:42	23
1:43	22, 24
1:45	24
1:46-48	23, 24
1:49	24
1:50	23
1:51	23, 24
2:1	22
2:11	23
8:19	73
12:45	73
14:7	73
20:29	23

Acts

13:47	28

26:18   28

Romans

10:4   59
13:1-7   81

1 Corinthians

7:20-24   81

11:2-15   81
14:33-35   81, 82

Galatians

1:15   28
3:24   59
3:28-29   82

Ephesians

5:31-32   82

1 Timothy

6:1-2   81

General Index

Amos, 55-56

Appropriation of meaning, 30-32, 34

Author, 16-17,19, 46, 82

Bible, 2, 8, 38, 43, 51, 62-64, 66, 72, 75, 81; pertinency, privileged, 63-64; rereading of 65; a single text, 56-58, 60, 62, 64, 81

Bultmann, Rudolf, 3, 9

Canon, 41, 43-45, 47-50, 71-72

Closure, 14, 15, 26, 32, 33, 36, 40-41, 43, 68, 80

Concordism, 6-7, 26

Conflict of interpretations, 31, 34, 39-40, 48

Context, 14

Darash, 5, 49, 89

Dead Sea scrolls, 48

Diachrony, 10, 48

Dilthey, Wilhelm, 3

Distantiation, 15-16, 20, 32, 34-35, 38

Dogma, 78, 79

Easter mystery, 53, 59

Ebeling, Gerhard, 3,9

Eisegesis, 66-68, 75, 89

Essenes, 31

Event, 36, 41, 45, 65, 71, 74-76, 77; originary, foundational, 37, 38, 39-40, 72

Faith, 72, 73, 77

"Forward" of a text, 50-53

Fuchs, Ernst, 3, 9

Fusion of horizons, 51, 89

Gadamer, H. G., 3, 51

God, 46, 52, 56, 63, 67, 72-74, 78, 80

Heidegger, Martin, 3

Hermeneutic circularity, 38, 70, 82

Hermeneutics, 1-2, 9-10, 11, 34, 45, 58, 64, 68-69, 72, 80, 81; biblical, 2; philosophical, 2-5

Hexateuch, 62

Historicism, 21, 26, 37

Historico-critical analysis, 7-9, 11, 26, 49

History, 8

Image, 78

Inerrancy, 46

Inspiration, 46-47

Interpretation, 29, 36-37, 39, 42, 75; involves enlargement of meaning, 1, 38; involves pre-understanding, 1, 3

Intertextuality, 43-44, 54, 55, 60, 82, 89

Intratextuality, 43-44, 46, 54-55, 60, 82, 89

Isaiah, 25, 30

Israel, 59-60, 63, 65, 66, 71, 78

Jamnia, Council of, 44

Jesus, 23-24, 29, 48, 53, 59, 60, 71, 73-75

Jewish canon, 44-45, 48, 57, 59

Judaism, 39, 44-45, 52, 59-60, 74-75

Kerygma, 44, 53, 58, 69-70, 78, 83

Kerygmatic axis, 53

Language, 10, 14, 20, 32, 45, 64, 78; and speech, 13-15; as text, 15-19

Latin America, 65, 76, 81

Leviticus, 59

Liberation, 39, 40, 52, 53, 56, 61, 65, 77

Liberation theology, 6, 33, 39, 67, 76, 80, 81

Marx, Karl, 31, 47

Matthew, 19

Meaning, 6, 20-21

Memory, 38

Midrash, 47, 49, 86n.23, 89

Myth, 78

Narrative semiotics, 54, 84n.11

Onomastic code, 23-24

Pashat, 5, 89

Paul, 18, 28, 49, 81-82

Pentateuch, 42, 44, 61-62

Pesher, 48, 49, 87n.29, 89

Philo of Alexandria, 4

Polysemy, 13, 15, 18, 26, 30, 32, 40-41, 80, 89

Power, 58-59

Praxis, 40, 45, 64-65

Present reality as "primary text," 5-6, 11

Preunderstanding, 1, 9

Production of discourse, 21-22

Production of meaning, 27, 30, 33, 50

Prophet, 73

Reading, 20-24, 25-26, 40

Receiver of a text, 17-18

Recontextualization, 79-80, 89

Referent of a text, 26-27, 90

Rereading, 32, 35, 46, 49, 57, 65, 66-68, 90

Reservoir of meaning, 32, 35, 38, 46-47, 50, 53, 56, 90

Revelation, 71-72, 74, 79

Ricoeur, Paul, 1, 3, 17

Schleiermacher, Friedrich, 3, 17

Semantic axis, 53, 58, 62, 64, 72, 79, 89

Semiotics, 10, 13-15, 80

Sense(s) of scripture, 4

Septuagint, 28, 29-30, 31, 32, 44-45

Social sciences, 80

Speech, 14-15, 20, 32, 45

Structural analysis, 9, 11

Symbol, 78

Synchrony, 10

Talmud, 47, 48, 60

Targum, 47, 48, 86n.23, 90

Targum of Jonathan (on Isaiah), 28, 31, 33

Text, 1, 16, 20-22, 32, 41, 43, 45, 46, 50, 71, 77, 80; basis of interpretation, 29-30

Torah, 73, 90

Tradition, 3, 4, 33, 41-43, 45, 48, 76

Upanishads, 47

Vedas, 31, 47

Word, 36, 41, 45, 68, 70

Yahweh, 52